Prescription for Living

Prescription for Living

by

Robert G. Wells, M.D.

HERE'S LIFE PUBLISHERS, Inc.

San Bernardino, California 92402

PRESCRIPTION FOR LIVING
by Robert G. Wells, M.D.

Published by
HERE'S LIFE PUBLISHERS, INC.
P. O. Box 1576
San Bernardino, CA 92402

Library of Congress Catalogue Card No. 83-047518
ISBN 0-89840-041-4
HLP Product No. 95-047-7

PRINTED IN THE UNITED STATES OF AMERICA

CONTENTS

Foreword

FOREWORD

PRESCRIPTION FOR LIVING relates the absorbing story of a prosperous and successful physician who at a young age achieved every goal he had set. He had tasted all the security of material comforts and basked in the luxury of the "good life." But he watched these fair-weather "friends" vanish when crisis struck, and then began to realize there was more to life than what he had been experiencing.

This book is more than a glimpse behind smock and stethoscope, more than just a doctor's testimony. It is a frank, hard-hitting, "nuts and bolts" synopsis of what Christianity really is.

For every Christian who wants to share his faith with family and friend, to tell him exactly what he believes, this is the ideal gift. For every person who has been looking for a palatable, easy to understand summary of how to find an intimate, close relationship with God, this book does the job.

We first met our friend, Dr. Bob Wells, several years ago in his Long Beach home where we were filming the movie, *Givers, Takers, and Other Kinds of Lovers.* In their foyer is an oak picture frame enclosing the beautifully cross-stitched words of Joshua which read, "As for me and my house, we shall serve the Lord." And this is what is happening in that home — a family serving God.

The spiritual leader of that family, and author of this book, is an obstetrician-gynecologist who has set a goal. He has committed himself to reaching personally more people with the gospel message than patients he has treated or babies he has delivered. And that's a lot! It may seem like an extraordinary task, but to know Dr. Wells and his unwavering faith in what God can do is to know also that this objective will be achieved.

As an obstetrician who has delivered literally thousands of babies, Dr. Wells knows all about the traditional hospital delivery room. But as a Christian physician, he also can speak with authority about God's "delivery room." In this book the reader will become acquainted with the obstetrical suite where new spiritual life begins. This unique delivery room is portrayed in the book as the exact site where each Christian-elect prays to receive Christ as Lord and Savior. For this reason it can be located anywhere . . . in a church, a park, an office, a car, the mountains . . . wherever new birth occurs and new life begins.

The entire book is built upon this obstetrical theme. Dr. Wells first describes step by step his own path to that delivery room where he found God and a changed life. Then he relates experiences of other people, including a number of his patients, some who enter their own spiritual delivery room and receive new life, and others who do not. Dr. Wells uses this analogy to compare these two great miracles of physical and spiritual birth, highlighting their striking similarities, and the reader learns exactly how every person can become a true Christian.

PRESCRIPTION FOR LIVING is powerful, moving, and poignant. It covers all the essential principles of Christianity in a clear, concise manner not easily forgotten. Be prepared to read non-stop, for it is not easy to put this book down once you have begun reading it.

JOSH AND DOTTIE McDOWELL

one

The Delivery Room of New Life

New life is no stranger to me.' As an obstetrician, I am privileged to be a part of the greatest and most stirring of all human events — birth.

I know quite a bit about this kind of new life. I have witnessed nearly every human reaction possible in a delivery room—including husbands passing out and couples openly fighting. I have watched incredible indifference on the part of expectant parents. I have winced at four-letter expletives from those who discovered that the girl they so desperately wanted turned out to be a boy.

My obstetrical world consists of both the routine and emergencies. I am called to perform Caesarean sections and to resuscitate newborns.

I have to treat maternal hemorrhage, shock, toxemia and even cardiac arrest.

But for me the greatest pleasure comes from the normal, joyful delivery (which takes place in the vast majority of cases), especially when the One who has made it all possible is given first credit.

One couple I recall did not forget to say thank you. Their story started in the labor room. I had just finished examining Cheryl. Beside her was a fetal monitor. Two lines marched across its graph paper. The bottom line recorded the increased pressure of amniotic fluid being squeezed every two to three minutes by contractions of the uterus. As the path of this line began its ascent, a noticeable stir of her body was quickly followed by the facial grimace of intense pain. The top ink line traced the baby's heart rate, a reassuring message from the tiny occupant inside.

"What is she now, Doctor?" asked the nurse standing nearby, poised to record the updated pelvic findings.

"Nine centimeters," I responded. "Nearly ready to move to the delivery room. It's also time for our expectant father here to climb into his scrub suit."

For the past several hours, Cheryl's husband, John, had been methodically rubbing his wife's back. His gentle voice and quiet manner were encouraging and comforting. As contraction followed contraction, her eyes, filled with strength and determination, remained fixed on what is called the focal point — an object designed to absorb a portion of the body's pain. This couple had selected a cross, which they had propped against a brown leather Bible on the nearby bedstand. I noticed that between pains she never forgot to smile reassuringly to her mate.

Obstetrics has certainly changed, I thought to myself as the nurse directed the expectant father to the dressing room. There he would change into the blue outfit that permits husbands to be an active participant in the delivery room. It was just a few short years ago that as a wife labored, her husband was a helpless spectator.

In those days, the delivery room was "off limits" to the father. Tradition assigned him to a smoke-filled waiting room with television blaring. There he sat imagining every horrible complication his wife might be experiencing at that very moment. They were separated, and she delivered *their* child in the midst of pain and strangers. Finally, after what seemed an eternity, the doctor would present himself at the waiting room door with a congratulatory smile and outstretched hand for the new father, announcing the baby's weight and sex.

In contrast, today's husband and wife become a team, actively using the principles of natural childbirth taught them during evening classes while their baby still floated in its dark, fluid-filled environment. In any course, some students are better than others. John and Cheryl had prepared themselves well.

As I stood there awaiting the nurse's return, I could see Cheryl's respirations begin to increase, but she was now in complete control. Several times earlier that evening, however, it had appeared as if the pain were becoming too much for her, and she had started to lose composure. But reassurance and persuasion from both husband and nurse helped her to reconcentrate on the principles learned and practiced during their natural childbirth classes.

"It's time to move you to the delivery room, Cheryl." My words broke the silence. The nurse returned and began to ready the patient for transport by gurney. John appeared in the doorway a few minutes later. His new outfit made him look "hospital" and professional, but his youthful apprehension belied that image.

In the delivery room, the dialogue between these two testified clearly to a solid marriage.

"Cheryl, you're doing just great! Look, Honey, you can see the baby's head." Both peered intently into the mirror that sent back a clear picture of the baby's head pressing against the resisting tissues of the vaginal opening. In the background, the fetal monitor continued to transmit its beep-beep-beep language of the fetus.

Not forgetting my role as part of this team, I added, "Now relax between contractions, Cheryl, to replenish your energy. That way you can push more effectively. With the next contraction, I want you to take two cleansing breaths and bear down. It's starting again. Ready? Take your breaths. Now push. Keep going. Longer. Keep pushing. Perfect."

I could hear John's voice from behind the mask counting — one, two, three, four, reaching fifteen before she gasped for another fill of air. To avoid a large tear, I injected a little local anesthetic in the area of the thin perineal skin and made a one-inch incision with the scissors. The spreading tissues then permitted the baby's head to appear over this episiotomy.

Kind of like a quarterback, I thought to myself, grinning behind the mask. Gently I gripped the newborn's head and guided it out of the birth canal. How many times had I done this, five thousand, six thousand? Yet, the whole aura surrounding each delivery still fascinates me.

"John, the head's out. Oh, John," Cheryl said. Still in total control and responding to each of my directions, she pushed, eased off, pushed again. The infant's left shoulder delivered beneath the pubic bone. Next the right shoulder, the trunk, and finally the buttocks slid smoothly into my hands. Almost in perfect unison as each saw the baby's "bottom" come into the mirror view, they shouted, "It's a girl!"

"Oh, John, it's a girl, it's a girl! Praise God! Thank You, Lord. Thank You, Lord, for giving us our child," cried Cheryl as the baby came to rest on her stomach at the moment of its first cry. No trumpet, no clarion ever sounded sweeter than the cry of that newborn to its parents.

Instinctively, Cheryl reached over and stroked her new daughter. John's eyes were moist as he kissed his wife through the mask. "A daughter, Cheryl, can you believe it? It's a miracle! Look at those tiny fingers. Is she all right, Doc?"

Following my reassurance that all parts were present and accounted for, his eyes once again gazed upon his new daughter. A family had been created — God's perfect plan.

The infant warmer was brought alongside the new mother while the nurse busily prepared the baby. The parents watched as medication was placed in each eye, then the umbilical cord was dabbed with a purplish antiseptic. Finally, the identification band was placed on the baby's foot, and an identical one was fastened around Cheryl's wrist.

Both John and Cheryl began to laugh and giggle as they saw their new daughter receiving her first medical attention. Noticing the white, greasy substance on her skin, John asked, "Is that the vernix, Doctor?" I nodded. *Chalk one up for him,* I thought. *He listened well in class.*

"It's a miracle!" That testimony has entered my ears more times than I could ever recount. The bustling hospital delivery room hosts those tender words. New mothers and new fathers alike utter them ecstatically. What a thrill it is to see tears of joy mist the eyes of new parents as they absorb every movement of their very own child.

A lusty cry declares to all the world that a perfectly coordinated plan has again resulted in the creation of a human being. The entire process, sending microscopic egg and sperm through the many stages to physical birth, can be described only as a miracle.

The Need for New Birth

"There is nothing more we can do for you, Margaret. No pills, no shots, no surgery. Nothing, absolutely nothing. I'm sorry."

The thirty-five-year-old patient sitting across from me in the consultation office looked more like fifty. Alcohol and cigarette pollution highlighted both skin and voice. Her aged face hard and resolute, she sought without success to hide anxiety and despair. Here was a human being at rock bottom.

"You've been my patient for a long time. I know what you've been through; I've watched what it's done to you. I've seen you look high and low for help, for answers – and each time come up short. Margaret, how about giving God a chance?"

A few years earlier, this now-distraught woman seemed to have every reason for happiness. She was vibrant, charming, and beautiful. Her circle of friends appeared limitless. Her husband, Michael, a lawyer, was both brilliant and ambitious. They had two children. Margaret entered into everything—PTA, Junior League, skiing, yacht club, even the community church. She and Michael merged perfectly into the city's social scene.

Then things began to change. About six years ago, she was in my office for an exam. She complained of feeling tired all the time. Both her physical examination and blood tests were normal.

At her next yearly visit, some new symptoms surfaced—headaches, backache, and vague abdominal pains. I suspected something was brewing.

"Margaret," I said to her, "your symptoms could be the result of a physical illness. But they could also be related to stress. We will be doing more tests, of course, but while we arrange for them, is there anything going on in your life now that might be causing these symptoms?"

I liked Margaret; she liked me; and in time a comfortable closeness often develops between doctor and patient. So without hesitation she began to talk. She allowed me to see inside the walls of her home, where her family was falling apart.

Michael never arrived home before 9 P.M. As his law practice and community prestige flourished, their marriage suffered. After a while, meaningful communication stopped; there was no feeling, no concern, no love for each other. They lost the vitality of their marriage. When together, they discussed only practical matters requiring decisions. They continued to attend all the parties, where each paired off with someone else. The drive home together was invariably a time of accusation and recrimination.

Teacher conferences at school served to make it clear that the children, too, were victims. Margaret and her husband had three separations, with intervening reconciliations effected primarily for the kids. With each restoration came something new — a sail boat, a car, even a new home. None touched the underlying disease.

Margaret found herself spending more and more time away from home and her children. She earned her real estate sales license and began to compete in the marketplace.

As she poured out her story, I only listened. I could see that was all she wanted me to do. Even an indirect reference to spiritual needs met abrupt resistance.

"I'm not into religion, Dr. Wells. That's not my bag." She smiled, but her words rang with seriousness.

Another year went by, another office visit. Independence, vanity, even bitterness had found their way to the surface. As Margaret brought me up to date, she voiced resentment toward her husband: "While he's out doing his thing, I'm left with the responsibility of raising the kids."

Their son, Mark, was under the care of a child psychiatrist. Daughter Debbie had become more and more sullen and withdrawn, often displaying wide mood variance. Margaret had wondered if Debbie might be using drugs. To top it off, the divorce proceedings approached completion.

Later, in the examination room, Margaret said, "What do you think of the *new* me, Dr. Wells?" She was obviously referring to her recent breast implants. The scars confirmed that the operation had been performed within the last few months, probably by one of the better plastic surgeons in Beverly Hills. The faint "crow's feet" that once flanked her eyes had also disappeared.

"Well, Margaret, surgically they did a great job. But has it helped you inside? Are you happier now?"

"I really am, Dr. Wells. I can date whomever I wish, whenever I wish. I am totally independent, and I love it. I should have done it years ago!" Her words were unconvincing.

Later, just before I started the pelvic examination, she murmured, "Oh, by the way, maybe you had better do a test for VD, just to be sure."

Since that feigned testimony of happiness, her life has been all downhill. The social whirl continued. Marijuana and cocaine frequently took the place of alcohol. To make matters even worse during those years, Margaret became obsessed with the thought that she had cancer. Convinced the dreaded diagnosis was being deliberately withheld from her, she consulted more than half a dozen medical specialists. No matter how many tests were run, and no matter how thorough they were, she remained unconvinced. Psychiatrists tried in vain to deal with the cancer phobia. Threats of suicide, even a weak gesture at pill overdose, complicated matters.

Despite all the grief caused by materialism, the pursuit of social position, drugs and sexual exploitation, she steadfastly refused to abandon these "friends," although it was obvious they were killing her.

From time to time, I continued to see her in the office. Sadly I witnessed this pitiful soul, drifting inexorably toward self-destruction. Her marriage was over, the children were confused and hurt, and her life was a shambles.

Now, sitting across the desk from me, thin, gaunt, but still determined, she listened quietly when I asked, "Margaret, how about giving God a chance?"

She just looked at me. Then she spoke, pathetically. "You may be right, Dr. Wells. God probably is the only one who can help me, if there is a God. But I'm not ready for that yet. It means giving up too much."

The Miracle of Births

Margaret is just one of the countless people being uprooted and torn apart. For them there can be only one solution—a whole new life. And that life must begin with birth of far greater significance than physical birth. It alone holds the ultimate power to heal. It is *spiritual* birth, or *new* birth.

Only one power is capable of restoring harmony to our lives. It is the power of God living in people. And it begins with the spiritual awakening called new birth. It is what Margaret needed. It is what we all need.

The greatest fact in the history of mankind is this: The almighty God of the universe actually can dwell within a person. Only this indwelling God can offer sanctuary in a chaotic world in which people are frantically looking for peace of mind. Only God in us can give hope and strength when simply coping becomes almost impossible.

This power, accompanying new birth, is able to shatter racial, cultural, and economic barriers, something man has never been able to accomplish with all his laws, welfare, and philosophies. It can do all this because it changes people from inside.

The "delivery room" for this special birth is truly different. Traditional delivery rooms are located in hospitals. But new birth, spiritual birth, takes place wherever one happens to be at the moment he calls out to God to take charge of his life. For some, this may be in a church sanctuary; for others, it can be in a living room, in the mountains, on a train, or in a pastor's study (as it was in my case).

God's "delivery room," where one is "born again," can be anywhere and any time, requiring only a place and a person. The person must first recognize the *need* for forgiveness, a need only God can satisfy. Next there has to be a *willingness* to surrender everything to Jesus Christ.

American Phrase?

In our country, the term "born again" once was heard only in revival meetings and evangelical churches. Then in the 1970s, the phrase suddenly erupted from quite unexpected places. High-ranking politicians, entertainers, athletes and even convicted criminals began to declare publicly that they had been "born again."

Critics mocked and laughed, calling it a crutch for the weak or "buying a rabbit's foot" for the strong. They dismissed it as a fad, a temporary phase that would leave as quickly as it came. As for the testimony of convicted criminals, the skeptics dismissed it as a ploy to win lenience in the courts.

Then things began to change. People became more tolerant, even curious. And in 1976 the American people heard Democratic Presidential candidate Jimmy Carter announce that he, too, was "born again."

The 1980s, however, have seen the molding of a new attitude toward spiritual birth. Atheists and agnostics have become more openly hostile to Christ and His cause. And so today the phrase "born again" finds itself battling for survival, the brunt of endless jokes and tasteless banter.

Why has the term stirred up so much controversy? What does "born again" mean? Who invented it? The expression is certainly not new — hardly a twentieth-century discovery. It was first used by a carpenter two thousand years ago.

Jesus of Nazareth, Himself the product of a unique pregnancy, claimed to be the Son of God. He spoke boldly about new life, life that could come only in the wake of new birth. In the third chapter of the Gospel of John in the New Testament, Jesus explains this obstetrical principle to a man named Nicodemus.

Nicodemus was the best that Judaism — even the whole world — could offer. He was a member of the highest-ranking group of Pharisees, the Sanhedrin, and was a leader who held a position of great esteem among his people. As a Pharisee, he was above reproach morally and ethically, a good man, a religious man, faithful and diligent in his prayer life. If anyone could earn a heavenly reward through total commitment, it would have been Nicodemus.

But to this righteous person, and to all the Nicodemuses of the world who think being good and working hard will get them into heaven, Jesus said, *"Unless you are born again, you can never get into the Kingdom of God"* (John 3:3, the Living Bible, emphasis added).

"Born again!" exclaimed the Pharisee. "What do you mean? How can an old man go back into his mother's womb and be born again?" (John 3:4,

TLB). The Jewish patriarch was confused. His logical mind pictured childbirth only as being bathed by maternal blood and amniotic fluid.

But Jesus was speaking of spiritual birth, a supernatural process leading to eternal life. John 1:12, 13 explains this second birth. *Rebirth simply means to ask and to receive Christ into our lives.*

Today the Lord might have said it another way: "Nicodemus, to get into heaven, you must do it *My* way, not yours. It means being born all over again, this time in a special 'delivery room' I have prepared for you. There you must ask Me to come into your life. I can't live there until you ask Me. I come by invitation only."

Nicodemus could not understand at that moment what was being said. It was too intangible, too abstract for his legalistic mind. Later, however, Nicodemus did experience that life-giving birth and became a follower of Jesus (see John 19:38–40).

Why and How of This Book

As a physician, I am totally convinced that spiritual birth is the only medicine effective against the spiritual aches and pains of life. It is both good-tasting and dependable. To recommend anything other than new birth to my patients for that malady which is the product of man's alienation from God is merely a waste of their time.

The assignment, then, is to make the prescription read as clearly as — and of course much more legibly — than the physician's handwritten instructions to the pharmacist. How could this be done?

The similarities between physical birth and spiritual birth are striking. What better way to write the prescription than by comparing the two! Being born again is the core, the very essence, of Christianity, but it is not complicated. Let me show you just how simple it is.

two

Spiritual Anatomy and Physiology

Exhilarating delivery room experiences climax to a series of events that have begun nine months earlier. Medical science is able to describe the anatomy and physiology of human reproduction, but it can never explain it. This is the way it transpires:

Each month the ovary, a small pelvic structure, hosts a sequence of grooming, preparatory events. Certain designated cells previously lying dormant near the surface of this ovary begin to stir. These cells coalesce to form a fluid-filled cavity that houses a tiny speck, the female egg.

Suddenly, at a predetermined time, the egg bursts free from its cystic chamber and into the abdominal cavity. It is lost for a while until the hovering Fallopian tube with its vacuum-like action grabs the ovum. The microscopic egg then wanders aimlessly down the tube's narrow channel.

To make matters even worse, this delicate organism is jarred and jostled by the action of the tube to the point that the very survival of the egg is in question. The bumpy migration is interrupted at about the middle of the tube, where, perhaps at the brink of demise, it encounters the life-giving male seed called the sperm.

One seed penetrates the egg, bringing the final and necessary ingredient. Life begins at this exact moment of conception.

The fertilized egg then completes its journey down the tube and into the cavity of the uterus. Here it finds a nourishing environment that will "feed" it for the next nine months.

Sometimes the uterine conditions are not favorable. Other times there are major intrinsic flaws in the new organism. Usually, when either of these things happens, the process comes to a halt with the product of conception being cast off in miscarriage early in pregnancy.

Most of the time, however, growth in the womb proceeds normally until one day a great tremor of involuntary forces begins and the muscular unit squeezes the baby down through the birth canal. Birth! The shock of the bright, new world is absorbed by the warm, cuddling arms of the baby's new guardians. All become acquainted in the delivery room.

From then on, at home, the baby begins to display remarkable changes as it grows. At first only able to digest milk, it soon requires more solid food. A proper and well-balanced diet is essential for growth.

Growing up is not easy. Love is vitally necessary; so is the tempering effect of discipline. Love is comforting; discipline is painful. As these two interact, an adult begins to emerge with the potential to parent a new generation. And the cycle repeats itself again and again and again.

A Trip to the Delivery Room

"... the ovary, a small pelvic structure, hosts a sequence of grooming, preparatory events. Certain designated cells previously lying dormant ... begin to stir."

Several years ago things began to "stir" in me. I found myself in the midst of a series of "grooming" circumstances destined to be my own "preparatory events." I did not know it then, but three seemingly unrelated developments would retrieve me from a spiritually "dormant" state and give new life through the miraculous process of spiritual birth. God had "designated" me and my family for His special gift. We were to be born again.

At first glance these developments may appear to have been mere coincidence. But closer appraisal and the passing of time confirmed that God even then was working in our lives.

The first preparatory event appeared after several years of medical practice. Inside, I began to ache — a vague feeling, hard to explain. Something was not right, and I knew it.

It was time for a thorough self-examination.

During the soul-searching that followed, I was forced to look at my priorities. I found them entirely materialistic. Happiness was the country club, the next vacation spot, a new car, an expensive home, flying my own plane. Not surprisingly, these topics always held top billing at the cocktail parties my wife and I regularly attended.

On the surface I was a successful young doctor, climbing from rung to rung, compiling an impressive record. But inside it was a different story. A bundle of fear, I was frightened of the future, frightened of illness, frightened of death.

Nothing seemed to assuage those fears. The more luxuries we acquired, the more problems were created. None of those possessions brought the expected return, but only turmoil and worry. Compounding the problem, I was dragging my wife and kids right along with me. The family unit was slowly disintegrating.

The second grooming incident occurred in the early months of 1970. "Is it a bone cyst or something else?" My voice trembled as I watched the radiologist carefully scan the X rays taken of my painful right ankle. My name was on the film not as the doctor, but as the patient. The adrenalin pumped through my body as I formed the words to the inevitable question: "Could it be cancer?"

The radiologist paused for what seemed an eternity. "I don't think so," he finally replied, "but it would be wise to get other opinions."

Fear and anxiety struck simultaneously.

Would my life be snuffed out by dreaded bone cancer? Surely it couldn't happen to me. I was too young. Those things happen only to other people. That day I fell apart emotionally.

The medical opinion on whether to operate was divided. Only a surgical biopsy would prove the true nature of the lesion. The majority of the orthopedists and radiologists consulted felt it was benign, so we decided against surgery.

Follow-up X rays confirmed the nonmalignancy, but I would never forget the panicky feeling enveloping me that afternoon as I stood frightened and stunned before the X ray view box. Like everyone else, during prosperous times I ignored the likelihood of death and judgment. But face to face with the possibility of dying, life suddenly took on new value.

Even more significant was the absolute failure of what I thought to be most important in life to comfort me in time of need. When I turned for help, where were those friends of mine – materialism, career, and personal pleasure? They were long gone – busy, no doubt, finding other victims.

As the ankle became stronger and X rays showed improvement, the third preparatory development surfaced. My wife, Mary, and I were both becoming concerned with the lifeless Sunday school the children attended at the neighborhood church. Each week they seemed to rebel more and more. Mary and I didn't go ourselves, of course. Nonattendance seemed easily justified: "I work hard all week. I deserve at least one day off..."

It upset us, however, that the children were not being challenged on Sundays. Someone suggested they might enjoy the program at a nearby church that had a strong children's emphasis. It also had a reputation for teaching the Bible.

We tried it. The kids grudgingly transferred to a new Sunday morning setting, expecting it to be more of the same. The change was not easy for us, either. Because of long-time loyalties to the community church, we felt almost like traitors. When the change was made, however, the results were phenomenal.

The three children actually began to enjoy and look forward to Sunday school. Next, my daughter, Julie, began to hit me with questions about the Bible that I couldn't begin to answer — most embarrassing. As the months passed by, it was astonishing to see remarkable changes in the behavior and attitudes of the children. We found it hard to believe.

Three grooming events began to turn my life in another direction. The emptiness of and dissatisfaction with my style of living, despite more and more material comforts, caused me grave concern. Next came a face-to-face confrontation with a life-threatening illness, evoking a sobering appreciation for what is really important in this world. Third, we experienced the simple need to locate our children in another Sunday school. These precursors ultimately would bring me to a spiritual awakening.

Lost and Found

"Suddenly, at a predetermined time, the egg bursts free from its cystic chamber and into the abdominal cavity. It is lost for a while until the hovering Fallopian tube with its vacuum-like action grabs the ovum. The microscopic egg then wanders aimlessly down the tube's narrow channel."

I was searching, with great need in my life. Certain questions had to be answered. Just like the egg "bursting free," I was "lost." Not knowing just where to turn, I found myself drawn to the same church that was responsible for the incredible changes in our children. A Bible-centered church would be the "tube," the "narrow channel" leading me to answers and new life.

The Rough Trip

"To make matters even worse, this delicate organism is jarred and jostled by the action of the tube to the point that the very survival of the egg is in question."

The search for personal peace and harmony was by no means comfortable. It was especially "jarring" to hear strange, illogical doctrine from the pulpit of that church —that doctrine was almost exactly opposite to everything I had come to believe.

On the other hand, I could not help but be impressed by the joy, enthusiasm and concern that radiated from the Christians there. They certainly had something I didn't have—a personal calm, a confidence that defied the frustrating realities of modern life.

Several things distinguished them. First, they called themselves "born-again Christians." Then, they carried their Bibles to church —and used them! They always gave God, not themselves, credit for everything. Neither weird nor fanatical, they were clean, well-dressed, solid citizens.

Few were wealthy, but all seemed spiritually rich. They said openly that their lives were not-problem-free—they had many difficulties, but God was always there to help them. How good that sounded. That's what I needed most, dependable help.

Strangely, I always had thought of myself as a Christian. I never doubted it, having grown up in a solid Christian home, raised by loving parents, both of whom knew Jesus Christ as their personal Savior. Their lives were living proof of the happiness and blessing that come with doing things God's way. But I just didn't see the need for going that far (rather, I didn't want to). I would rest on my parents' faith and do things my own way.

My philosophy seemed quite rational. Jesus was just another great man. His moral teachings were praiseworthy, but hardly applicable in today's complex society. Naturally, I adopted some scriptural standards, but I discarded those having no specific appeal, especially those conflicting with my life-style.

Sin, by *my* definition, was something that hurt someone else. I was free to do anything I wanted as long as it did not harm others. I was skeptical about life after death. If there were a heaven, it was reserved for those who lived a moral, golden-rule-type life. Hell could be only right here on earth—the painful consequences that accompany being "bad." A God of love would surely never punish anyone for eternity.

That was my code, and I held to it tenaciously. From a practical standpoint, it was designed to give maximum liberties without overtaxing the conscience — a neat little package, yet both frustrating and discouraging. Many mornings I would vow to "turn over a new leaf," yet hours or even just minutes later, I would be back into my old ways. New resolutions were so common as to be routine.

But the bubble burst when my own philosophy was pitted against that of Scripture, which I was then hearing from the pulpit of the new church. *How could my values have strayed so far from the Bible's?* I asked myself.

My thinking processes were really being "jostled" by this sharp contrast. As it frequently does, doubt quickly followed. Perhaps what I was hearing was false. After all, the Bible could be interpreted in many different ways. Maybe their impression was wrong. Possibly I should keep looking elsehwere.

The Seed

"The bumpy migration is interrupted at about the middle of the tube, where, perhaps at the brink of demise, it encounters the life-giving male seed called the sperm. One seed penetrates the egg, bringing the final and necessary ingredient. Life begins at this exact moment of conception."

I was about to reject it all, "on the brink of demise," when something clicked. I couldn't explain it, it just all suddenly seemed right. Personal testimonies of Christians made the difference. They openly discussed how Jesus Christ of the Bible had changed their lives. Firsthand results of that change could be seen. Inside, I knew what they were saying was true.

Each story had one common denominator, a biblical plan called the gospel. The gospel is that "penetrating seed." When I first heard it clearly outlined, I sensed it might just change my life. It did more than that; it gave me *new* life.

Before it was explained, I had no idea what the gospel was. Oh, I had heard of gospel hymns, gospel singers, and, of course, gospel preachers. Who in America hadn't? For all I knew, the gospel was just an oozy sermon from the lips of one of those emotional, silver-tongued preachers.

When I discovered that the word *gospel* is an English equivalent for the Greek word meaning *good news* it occurred to me that I was ready for some good news. That welcome message was that God offers eternal life as a gift. "And the witness is this, that God has given us eternal life" (1 John 5:11).

The gospel message, I learned, is simply God's blueprint for a fulfilling life here on earth —Jesus said, "I came that they might have life, and might have it abundantly (John 10:10) —*plus* guaranteed life after death. God not only created man, but also to every human being He offers the opportunity to spend eternity with Him. The apostle Paul spoke of the prospect of being "absent from the body and ... at home with the Lord" (2 Corinthians 5:8).

To receive this great prize, all we have to do is be perfect! "Human being," God says, "to live with Me, you must be like Me, absolutely perfect, holy, without sin." Now, you don't have to be a Rhodes scholar to see the dilemma in that kind of an arrangement. And it is hardly "good news."

God knows man is not sinless; He knows we are not perfect. "All have sinned and fall short of the glory of God" (Romans 3:23). "There is none who does good, there is not even one" (Romans 3:12). The word *sin* in the Greek New Testament (the original language of the N.T.) comes from the ancient sport of archery and means "to miss the mark," the bull's eye of God's perfection. And it makes no difference to God whether we miss that mark by a little or a lot, by one sin or a million (James 2:10).

But God's supernatural love is seen clearly in the solution built into His seemingly impossible requirements. God Himself became a man, Jesus. Still possessing His divine nature (John 10:30; 14:9), His mission was to live the perfect and sinless life man is incapable of living. Then Jesus went voluntarily to the cross in our place. Along with the nails and the torture, He took with Him every sin of man—past, present, and future. As the apostle Paul said, "For God took the sinless Christ and poured into him our sins" (2 Corinthians 5:21, TLB). His death was payment in full for the sentence actually belonging to us.

With the penalty, spiritual death (Romans 6:23), paid once and for all, we can now be judged not guilty. With the penalty paid, there is no case against us. Innocent of our sin, we can stand perfect before God. Innocent of sin, we are awarded eternal life with Him.

Neat and simple, right? But there are terms. To receive this kind of pardon, to allow Jesus to "take the rap" for us, we must first believe by faith that it all happened just that way. Second, we must act on that belief by asking Jesus Christ into our life.

That's it. That is the gospel, the Lord's plan for mankind. God wants to inseminate every human being with this seed. It is the greatest love story ever written. "For God so loved the world, that He gave His only begotten Son, that whoever believes in Him [Jesus] should not perish, but have eternal life" (John 3:16).

The "seed" brings new spiritual life "at this exact moment of conception." But true Christianity is more than just believing. Others must know about the agreement between you and God. The audible cry of the newborn must be heard. Although new life may exist, it is not evident to the world until the baby actually is born. In God's delivery room, each believing person must confess with his mouth that Jesus is exactly who He claimed to be, God in human flesh (Romans 10:9). All this I learned.

Growth in Preparation for Birth

"The fertilized egg then completes its journey down the tube and into the cavity of the uterus. Here it finds a nourishing environment that will 'feed' it for the next nine months."

For me, the subsequent months were spent being "fed." For the first time in my life, I became acquainted with the Bible. For hours I talked to one of the pastors, Charlie Beatty, a faithful and dedicated man of God. He encouraged me to read and discover for myself how this great book deals specifically with each question I was asking. Gently and patiently, he met my skepticism.

Stubbornly, I continued to resist. The philosophy of the world had been thoroughly ingrained in me. It seemed very logical that a man

by his hard work could earn his way to heaven.
Yet the Bible declared that a man could never earn
his way to heaven no matter how hard he worked.

According to Ephesians 2:8, 9, "For by grace
you have been saved through faith; and that not
of yourselves, it is the gift of God; not as a result
of works, that no one should boast." To make the
message even clearer, Titus 3:5 adds, "He saved
us, not on the basis of deeds which we have done
in righteousness, but according to His mercy."
When we try to make our way into heaven on our
own merits, God calls our futile efforts "filthy
rags" (Isaiah 64:6, KJF).

For about nine months, this doubter spent his
time trying to discredit the Bible's authenticity,
message and application. During many sessions
in the pastor's study, the skeptic pointed out the
"flaws" of Christianity.

My Delivery Room

"One day a great tremor of involuntary forces
begins and the muscular unit squeezes the baby
down through the birth canal. Birth!"

Finally, I ran out of side-stepping excuses and
objections, realizing the imbalance of my
priorities. I could never forget my panicky
response to the threat of cancer. A vivid lesson
had been learned. When my life seemed in jeop-
ardy, everything I had once thought important—
and capable of holding me up in all situations—
let me down.

One thing was clear: Doing it my way had been a disaster. When this doctor took his own spiritual pulse, he found it too slow even to maintain life.

Then I became conscious of "involuntary forces" bringing me to a decision. The Bible made it clear what had to be done.

For months I had remained cautious and deliberate. Now, looking back, I believe part of that hesitancy was making sure this was not just a passing fancy or another stage in my life. Going public was serious business.

On September 10, 1971, I surrendered my life to Jesus Christ. Telling Him I was giving up, I asked Him to save me. That day He and I established a binding, intimate relationship.

It was a humbling experience; the ego had to be beaten into submission. But that was a reasonable price to pay for finding a life worth living. Humility, indeed, is the key to unlocking the power of God.

That day, sitting in the study of Charlie Beatty, my heart and my lips both acknowledged the truth of the gospel. The two of us went over again the Bible's assertion that faith in Christ is the only way to God's salvation. Jesus Himself said, "I am the way, and the truth, and the life; no one comes to the Father, but through Me" (John 14:6). The apostle Peter added, "There is salvation in no one else; for there is no other name under heaven that has been given among men, by which we must be saved" (Acts 4:12).

"Well, Charlie," I said, "it boils down to one thing. In order to be born again, I'm going to have to invite Christ into my life. Right?"

"That's right, Bob," my pastor said. "Everyone must do it. There are no exceptions. The Lord will not invade your life without an invitation. Having believed in His death for your sins, you must receive Him, reach out to Him in a total commitment of your life."

"Well, it doesn't make complete sense to me, but if that's what God says, then let's do it. One thing for sure, doing it my way isn't working. I think I'd better give God a shot at it."

My prayer was a little awkward, but I meant what I said. Without any big emotional scene, I had a good feeling, an assurance I had at last done the right thing.

Emerging a true Christian, I had received the greatest gift of all. I had been born again, with the pastor's study as my "delivery room."

Later, I discussed this commitment and prayer with my wife and children. Three months later, as a Christian family, we were baptized together in obedience to God's command, a public testimony to our new "indwelling tenant."

Christian Growth

"From then on, at home, the baby begins to display remarkable changes as it grows. At first only able to digest milk, it soon requires more solid food. A proper, well-balanced diet is essential for growth."

From that moment, I discovered what a partnership with the living God could do in the growth department. Instinctively I wanted to learn more about God's Word. That was not surprising, for the Bible predicts that newborn believers will have a new appetite (1 Peter 2:2). The wisdom and insights of the Bible constantly amazed me. *What took you so long to find this treasure?* I kept asking myself.

Other changes became evident, too, not abruptly but clearly surfacing as time passed. The spiritual metamorphosis brought a different person with a different life-style. "Therefore if any man is in Christ, he is a new creature; the old things passed away; behold, new things have come" (2 Corinthians 5:17).

Like dead leaves randomly falling from a tree, most of the former pleasures no longer interested me. A few of them stubbornly still cling, but I know God will take those away, too.

Because of verses like Hebrews 2:15, fears about death and the future, once so prominent in my life, stopped haunting me. This "worry wart" began to worry much less. No longer on that treadmill going nowhere, I found life full of meaning and purpose.

Growth meant taking the Lord to work with me each day. At the office, in the hospital—the delivery room and operating room—He was always there, the faithful source of wisdom and confidence. When patients ached spiritually and emotionally, it was God's wisdom I offered, not mine.

My growth was also reflected in our social lives. Inevitably our circle of friends changed. Some of them referred to us as getting very religious. Many of them continued to worship the false, humanistic gods of today, not realizing it is idolatry. Others, however, began to question that type of living. We are now trying to remain on call to help them, praying that they, too, might find their way to God's delivery room.

Growing also meant learning what foods provided the best nourishment. It did not take long to see the importance of daily prayer, daily Bible study, regular church attendance, and other Christian fellowship. That is the "proper, well-balanced diet" necessary for Christian growth. When I stuck to this diet I was happy. When I became "too busy" for these important foodstuffs, problems brought turmoil.

Next, this growing infant learned a lot about priorities. Mine had been fouled up too long. The Bible helped me list the proper order:

1. God
2. Wife and children (in that order)
3. Church attendance and fellowship with other Christians

4. Job and career
5. Personal amusements and material things

Previously, career and personal amusements had crept to the top of my list. The consequence of improper priorities is always disaster, and I had been heading down that path.

God's Bonus

That decision of September 10, 1971, had a colossal impact on my marriage. Once uncommunicative and materialistic, my wife and I now enjoy a new excitement, a new accord. We fell in love again. Mary is no longer just my wife, but my closest friend as well.

Scripture again provided the formula that made this new relationship possible. And why shouldn't it? After all, God did create man and woman. Certainly He would be the best counselor on the subject of marriage. True, we still have problems from time to time. We recognize Christianity is not a problem-free life. But we let God do the mending.

The Bible clearly defined each of our roles in marriage and in the family. As husband, I was first charged with the responsibility to love my wife (Ephesians 5:25). That sounds simple enough, but real love is commitment to meet all her needs – spiritual, emotional and physical.

The Bible says a man is really doing himself a favor when he loves his wife. How true! Consider the emotional trauma and financial predicaments that follow in the wake of a divorce. All those could be avoided if people would just let God build their homes.

Second, the Bible demanded that I honor my wife (1 Peter 3:7). She is my equal; I am commanded to hold her in highest esteem and treat her in a manner worthy of her position.

Third, I was to teach and guide her in spiritual things. God commands the husband to be the spiritual head and teacher of the family; He would minister to Mary and the children through me. That was a scary responsibility. I had to get closer to God, and that meant earnestly studying His Scriptures.

Before long the Bible became our family "rule book," the final authority. It provided insights, suggestions and guidelines for every aspect of our family living. "Milk" made way for more "solid food" as we became more intimately acquainted with its contents.

Mary rejoiced to see the adjustment in roles. Her stamp of approval was reflected in a changing attitude toward me. Some would object to Scripture's "chain of command." They fear that designating the husband as head of the family means the wife becomes a second-class citizen.

But marital submission God's way never leads to any form of slavery. The more Mary responded to my new role, the more love I wanted to give back to her. This biblical relationship stifled neither her personality nor her identity—just the opposite. Protected from outside responsibility, free of the burden of authority, she burst forth with new confidence, new creativity.

Our union is ten times what it used to be, and all because we read and follow God's handbook on marriage. When His principles are adopted in any husband-wife relationship, that marriage will flourish.

The Challenge of Children

We noticed that as our marriage improved, the family also grew closer. That is not surprising, for the most important thing a father can do for his children is to love their mother. Children absorb the attitudes, tensions, joys and anxieties that fill the home.

Ephesians 5 and 6 are "family chapters." They declare that children are to obey their parents, for it is the right thing to do (6:1). Whenever this passage was read at the dinner table, my kids always pointed out another verse: "Fathers, do not provoke your children to anger" (6:4). A little something for everyone!

Paul's letter to the Ephesians caught our eye at just the right time. Finding it difficult, almost impossible, to be parents of teenagers, we thought those years had to be the most exasperating of all. Raising young children is physical exhaustion; but raising teenagers is physical *and* mental exhaustion. Every parent who gets through those years deserves a special award. Again, the Bible provided the much-needed comfort, wisdom and encouragement to survive.

In our home, we try to give the Lord the seat of honor. Anyone can build a house, but only He can build a home. He offers the greatest homeowner's policy ever written—and its premiums are free!

Discipline in Growth

"Growing up is not easy. Love is vitally necessary; so is the tempering effect of discipline. Love is comforting; discipline is painful."

My new life also brought frustration and disappointment. God had given me so much, yet how often I let Him down. Each occasion was a lesson, pointing out clearly my dependence on Him. Left on my own, I would always revert to infancy.

Eight years after becoming a Christian, I demonstrated that perpetual weakness at a time when pride of spiritual accomplishment was beginning to get a foothold in my thought life.

"You _____!" I yelled from behind my surgical mask. Things were not going well in the operating room that morning.

The scrub nurse, herself a Christian, appeared visibly shaken. "Doctor Wells, I can't believe you said that!" she said.

I couldn't believe it, either, yet it obviously came from me. In a thoughtless moment I had hurt a fellow believer, damaged any prior Christian credibility I might have had with others in the operating room, and horrified myself. Although depressed and mourning over that incident for days, I did learn to get my eyes back on God. Smugness and pride have no place in the life of a believer. Any goodness that appears in our lives is there only because of the grace of God.

Growth Toward Reproduction

"An adult begins to emerge with the potential to parent a new generation. And the cycle repeats itself again and again and again."

Sitting in the locker room of the athletic club that morning, the profanity seemed even more profuse and offensive than usual.

"_____! You couldn't miss today."

The voice came from Hank, sitting across the room, holding a glass of beer. Four handball players at his table were indulging in the usual postgame laments.

Pete and I were sitting at a table alone. The sweat was still dripping.

"Do you know Him?" I asked Pete, referring to the name Hank had used as an expletive.

"Know who?" Pete looked over at me.

"Know Jesus Christ?" I said.

"What are you talking about, Wells?"

"Hank over there just used Jesus' name. Listen, it won't be long until he uses it again." I paused a minute. Sure enough, out it came. Then I continued, "You know, Pete, Jesus' name is used more in this club than in a church." I paused a minute. "Well, *do* you know Him?"

"Come on, Wells, he was just cussin'! _____, no, I don't know Him. Who does?"

"Pete, I know Him. Come on, let's grab a jacuzzi"

Pete and I had become good friends since we began playing racquetball together. Now we walked back and sat in the whirlpool. He had been married once and divorced. His former wife had custody of their two children. Since the divorce, life had become one party after another. He was drinking far too much. Once, he told me, he was so drunk that he woke up the next morning in the middle of a residential street. Total amnesia eclipsed the events of the previous night, and that really worried him.

Everyone liked Pete. His personality was infectious. He looked like the All-American boy — blond hair, blue eyes, and a million-dollar grin. But lately he had been depressed, really down. His girlfriend had just left him, calling his life a waste. Pete took it hard. The weeks that followed were filled with brooding and more drinking.

As we talked, the hot, circulating water felt good against my aching muscles. Pete began to reveal a personal side that previously had been hidden. "You know, Bob, this fun-and-games stuff is a sham. I am really hurting."

Two days later we had lunch together, and he gave me the opportunity to discuss Jesus with him. There was nothing fancy, just the facts about who Jesus was and how He had helped me and my family.

"Pete," I said, "is something inside telling you that what I'm saying is true?"

"Yeah, but I can't be one of those religious fanatics. That isn't my style," he replied.

"God doesn't want you to be a 'fanatic.' He wants you to be yourself, but He also wants to use you for His special purpose." Smiling, I continued, "Maybe He wants you to be the best racquetball player in the world."

Pete's spiritual delivery room was his own bedroom. One night, all alone, he prayed to commit his life to Christ. Two months later in a small church, Mary and I watched his baptism. I've never seen a person change so dramatically. The spark, the grin, all came back. Happiness is written all over his face — and no more booze. His appetite for Scripture seems never satisfied, and he is discipling other new Christians every Tuesday morning.

Pete's own mother received Christ as Lord and Savior as a direct result of his clear testimony, both from his lips and from his new life. His friends still can't believe what happened.

Now each time I see Pete, I'm reminded how

God's great gift can truly change people. I see firsthand "a new generation," and the "cycle repeats itself again and again and again."

three

His Book

Every hospital maintains strict rules and regulations directing the operation of its delivery room. These are written and enforced by experienced people for the smoothest operation of the room and the safety and well-being of all who use it.

In a similar way in the spiritual realm, there is a guidebook, a list of directions, given for the safety and well-being of everyone. It was written under the inspiration of God, the designer and creator of everything. It is, of course, the Bible. Those who accept its authority and live according to its teaching in the power of the Holy Spirit can experience the fullest, most satisfying life possible.

As different people come to God through Christ, however, they come at different levels of understanding of His Word. I had been a skeptic, and before I would commit my life to the God revealed in the Bible, there were some questions about that Bible for which I had to have satisfactory answers. Was the Bible trustworthy? Was it dependable? Was it true? And most importantly, was it actually God's Word?

Nothing Is Absolute?

One day in our office, my partner and I laughed about some of the contradictions of modern science. A new report had just been released indicating that saccharin was safe after all. A research team from a prestigious medical center had announced that it was unable to confirm studies done three years earlier that had found saccharin to be a cancer-causing chemical. The new research showed the sugar substitute to be safe, possibly even beneficial.

"Can you believe it?" I commented in astonishment. "Whatever is fact today is just the opposite tomorrow."

My associate grinned in agreement. "Seems there are no absolutes," he said.

Wrong, I later thought to myself. *There is one absolute, one ultimate and final authority — the written Word.* Unfortunately, man too often fails to recognize it as such, despite God's caution that our "faith should not rest on the wisdom of men, but on the power of God" (1 Corinthians 2:5).

I had not always believed that. As I read the

Bible seriously for the first time, my mind also carefully assessed the extent of its authority. The book made a bold statement: it said God was its author. The words "Thus saith the Lord" are found more than two thousand times in the Old Testament. Jesus Himself gave His stamp of approval to Scripture when He quoted from nearly all the Old Testament books in a manner indicating He considered it the final word on *every* subject.

Bible critics disagree. How could it be God's revelation to man when it was written by man himself? It is popular for "side-steppers" to begin by questioning both its accuracy and its application.

"It's just a matter of interpretation."

"Don't be silly. You can't take the Bible literally!"

"The meaning of the Bible has changed in the various translations, and having been written so long ago, it has to be inaccurate. Just think of all the errors that have crept in over the centuries."

"Things are different today. The Bible no longer applies."

"You don't believe Adam and Eve actually existed, do you?"

Remarks like these usually come from someone who hasn't read the Bible. How well I know, because I was once one of them, repeating the same rhetoric. Side-steppers are "experts" on a subject they know nothing about.

Do you have questions or reservations about the world's best-selling book? Then read it for yourself. Don't fall into the trap of echoing the hollow criticisms of those unqualified "experts." *Decide for yourself* if God is truly the author.

For those who find the poetic "thee"-and-"thou"-style of the King James Version difficult to understand, one of the excellent modern translations or paraphrases will prove helpful. *The Living Bible,* the *New International Version,* and the *New American Standard Bible* are just a few examples of today's readable and conservative versions.

One may begin by reading the New Testament book of John. One of the twelve disciples, John describes the life of Jesus and the purpose of His mission to earth. He was the closest of all to the Lord, and he came to realize that the humble carpenter was, indeed, God in human flesh.

Chance, Collaboration, or One Author?

One of the strong arguments for the authenticity and divine nature of the Bible is its unity. Did you know that the sixty-six books of the Bible were written by more than forty different men representing all walks of life? Some were kings, some philosophers, some poets, some scholars, some fishermen, and one even a physician. They lived in different regions and wrote in three separate languages over a period of sixteen hundred years. Yet in all their writings there is perfect harmony, with no significant contradictions. It all fits together like a giant puzzle. How is this possible?

Just imagine forty doctors, writing independently over a period of sixteen hundred years, compiling a textbook on the causes and treatment of disease. Picture the countless medical theories and superstitions of sixteen centuries included in the same text with modern-day medical knowledge. What a hodgepodge book it would be!

The literary harmony of the Bible could not be pure chance. Nor could it be a conspiracy of its many writers. There is another, simple explanation: one author – God Himself. The Holy Spirit selected, inspired and used each penman to write exactly what He intended to communicate to us. "Men spoke *from* God as they were carried along by the Holy Spirit" (2 Peter 1:21, NIV, emphasis added).

Prophecy – Further Proof

If all the predictions found in biblical prophecy came true exactly as foretold, it would be a powerful argument for the reliability of Scripture. Is biblical prophecy accurate?

As just one example of how accurate it is, indeed, consider that the Old Testament continually prophesied the coming of a Savior, detailing more than three hundred facts about the promised Messiah. And Jesus fulfilled them all.

Some of those prophecies included the exact place and circumstances of His birth; the nature of His ministry; His betrayal and its exact price; the manner of His death; His last spoken words; and, most importantly, His bodily resurrection.

Comparing with the Classics

Another strong argument for the reliability of an ancient literary work such as the Bible comes from being able to establish that the existing manuscripts from which our English versions are translated are faithful to the original manuscripts. We have no original biblical texts, just as there are also no original texts of such other ancient works as Homer's *Iliad*.

To make a good case for the faithfulness of those existing manuscripts to the originals, two things are helpful. First, the more copies of the manuscripts you have, the better you can establish that they do (or don't), in fact, accurately reflect the originals. And second, the older the manuscripts are that you have—that is, the closer the time of their copying was to the time they were originally written—the more likely they are to be faithful to the originals and the less chance there is that error has crept in over the centuries.

Comparing the Bible to other ancient classics on these two criteria, then, we find that there are only 10 manuscript copies of Caesar's *Gallic War*, with some 900 years intervening from the time of the original document to our oldest available copy. There are 49 ancient manuscripts of each of Aristotle's works, with a 1,400-year interval between the oldest of them and the original writing. Homer's *Iliad,* considered the most "sacred" nonreligious piece of literature today, has 643 ancient manuscript copies.

In contrast, there are more than 24,000 surviving manuscripts of the New Testament, and some of the best copies were written within 100 to 300 years of the original writings. Therefore, to question the reliability of the Bible in terms of its faithfulness to the original texts is to question or even discard as unreliable all the classic works of literature. No one seems willing to do that. But there have always been those wanting to discredit the Bible. Why does it find itself under constant abuse and attack? Why do people fear it so?

We Stand Naked

The Bible is in one sense the most difficult of books to read, because no other book in the world exposes our true motives or judges our innermost thoughts, like the Bible. Thus, reading the Bible can be a very uncomfortable experience. That is why so many have tried to discredit it. It may be why the Bible is the world's *least read* best seller.

A small boy, looking up to the top shelf of a closet at a dusty and discolored black Bible, once asked: "Whose book is that, Mommy?"

She was startled. "Why, that's God's book," she said.

The child's response was a frank indictment of the human race: "Well, why don't we give it back to God? We never use it!"

Knowing the Author

A friend and I had just finished playing racquetball. On the back of a T-shirt I wore that day was a large Bible with the words "SURVIVAL KIT" scrawled across it.

Sitting in the locker room, my friend pointed to my shirt and said, "You know, Wells, I've read some of the Bible, but I can't get into it. I don't want to hurt your feelings 'cause I know you're religious and all that stuff, but I found it boring. Why is everyone making such a big deal about it lately?"

I told him a story Bill Bright of Campus Crusade for Christ relates about a young woman whose friends once told her about a famous novel. Intrigued, she bought the book and began to read it. However, she was quickly disappointed and found it difficult to stay with the book. She would read for a while, then put it down. Later, she would pick it up and try again when her friends kept telling her what a marvelous book it was. They told her over and over to keep trying. But soon she ceased to read it.

One day she met the author of the book. They began to date. She fell deeply in love with him, and they were soon married. After the wedding, she picked up the same book and began to read it again. To her amazement, she now discovered that it was the most exciting book she had ever read. It wasn't long before she, too, was recommending it to *her* friends. What was the difference? *She knew the author.*

That is precisely what happens today. People who have not yet become Christians will frequently find the Bible difficult to understand and, as in the experience of my racquetball-playing friend, just plain dull. The Bible itself says that the unbelieving world will find it foolishness (1 Corinthians 1:18).

The reason? Unbelievers have never become acquainted with the divine writer, and that is the key. The Bible speaks to those who know the author, and He is found only in a specially tailored delivery room, one carefully chosen for each Christian-elect.

The Perfect Standard

How shall we live? What measure, what standard, do we then follow? What source explains the sense of life? Even its most cynical critics concede that the Bible presents an exceptional code of ethics. So why must we look for alternatives? In today's society young people are confused, and why not? The adult world seems bent on scrapping God's book of life, leaving children with no consistent standard to tell them what is right and wrong. Little wonder they fall quickly for the foolishness that something must be right if it feels good.

How fortunate we are to have the written word as the ultimate yardstick. What if we had no Bible and had to determine truth solely from human reasoning? The logic of one person could always be challenged by the logic of another. Who would decide what to include and what to leave out? There would be no objective standard of truth against which to check the evil tendencies of humanity.

To avoid the chaos that would invariably arise if God had not spoken, God in His infinite grace has given us His book. Perfect in its content, the Bible spares us from wallowing in a maze of bickering and controversy as we search for wisdom and truth. How thankful we should be to have a God to set rules for human conduct.

Faith – The Final Proof

Do Christians believe God wrote the Bible only because of the accuracy of its fulfilled prophecy, its literary unity, the reliability of its existing manuscripts, or the countless archaeological discoveries that have verified its historical accuracy? No, only one way leads ultimately to belief in His authorship – faith, and faith alone in the Bible's claim that "all Scripture is inspired by

God" (2 Timothy 3:16).

Once a person risks that step of faith, however, the content of Scripture rewards him with even more faith. Spiritually, it is part of a victorious, not a vicious, circle. Faith unlocks the truths of Scripture, and the truth unveiled leads to more assurance and faith – for more unlocking.

The Bible's unity, consistency and practical application to every facet of life excite the Christian. He savors its knowledge and uses its wisdom. He knows it is the best source and final test of truth. For two thousand years it is the one book that has done, does, and will do the job.

four

Doing It Our Way

The Bible is emphatic. We must have two births, one physical and one spiritual. Human philosophy disagrees. It insists that physical birth equips us with all the necessary resources to find happiness. It claims man needs no spiritual delivery room.

But human philosophy is really nothing more than human instinct, and instinct is simply *doing it our way.*

Movies, television, newspapers, magazines, psychiatrists, and authors nudge us along the world's way to fulfillment. And it all seems so right, because each person gets to choose his own way. The world's system portrays happiness as material comforts and personal pleasures — homes, cars, parties, vacations, etc. Happiness is accomplishment, reaching the top of the ladder.

Happiness can be found in education or religion. And with brainwashing regularity, we are told that happiness is being "turned on" by sex and physical beauty. The list of purported ways to find peace of mind is unending.

Barbara's Way

Doctors have favorite patients. Barbara is one of mine. She has pursued at least three commonly chosen pathways in her own search for identity and security.

Barbara is mature, intelligent, soft-spoken and confident. In her mid-forties, she has a distinctive natural beauty. Her eyes are a soft gray, and there are touches of matching color in her lovely brown hair. Her smile is warm and personable. Delicately built, she is the picture of femininity.

Barbara's life has not been easy. But you would never know it by looking at her. In fact, one of the things I most admire about her is her composure. She is always in total control.

During her senior year in college she married Don, a serious, enterprising, young business graduate. After many interviews, he chose a large Southern California corporation in which to launch his career. The executives of that company saw in Don the talent and ambition to carry him to the top. They were right. Fifteen years later that's just where he was, but not without cost.

In his quest for corporate achievement, he spent less and less time with Barbara and their three children. Don found it increasingly more difficult to make it to his daughter's gymnastics matches and his son's Little League games. Barbara had to represent him at PTA and Scout meetings, and finally even at "family" vacations. All this happened while the social side of *his* business calendar burst at the seams and recorded 100 percent attendance. Don became a workaholic, hungry to make it big, determined to provide himself and his family with financial security.

For Barbara, the buying power of his ever-increasing salary cushioned the pain of his absence. There was a beautiful home on the sixteenth fairway of the country club to which they belonged, a Palm Springs condominium, two Mercedes, expensive clothes and jewelry, tennis, golf and luncheons. This was all very exciting to Barbara, who had never known such a side of life, and it satisfied her for many years. And yet I was impressed by how little all this affected her. Wealth can easily destroy, but Barbara was not one of its victims.

In the midst of all this financial security, however, Barbara and Don went to court. Irreconcilable differences were the two words that granted them legally separate lives.

Don remarried. Barbara did not. Apart they finished raising the children the best they could. With money and luxuries no longer as plentiful, she searched for new challenges. She resurrected a dormant artistic talent that had been shelved during her married life. She found excitement in sculpturing. Working in bronze, she did mostly infants and children, and sold many of her fine pieces. The bulk of her days and evenings was spent at the art department of the nearby state college. Her talents immediately caught the attention of her professors, who encouraged her to go back to school. She did and even began teaching. In two years she was an assistant professor. She thrived in this academic arena. Seminars, tours and art shows stimulated her anew. They satisfied important needs.

She came into contact with many other artists and soon became a part of their culture. It wasn't long before her own life-style began to take on a distinct Bohemian flavor.

One of her artist friends introduced her to Transcendental Meditation (TM). One meeting was all it took. Next there were trips to TM centers throughout the country, including the Maharishi International University in Iowa. Her home became a local meditation center. She was hooked. Teaching and sculpturing had lost their zing.

At one of her office visits, she was wearing a gold pendant on a necklace. I commented on the pendant's attractiveness. She turned it over. On the opposite side was a portrait of her guru.

"Barbara, tell me about Transcendental Meditation," I said. "I know it has become a very important part of your life, and it's now very popular in the United States, isn't it?"

For the next half hour she told me about her new-found source of strength.

"I know many people would not understand," she said. "Some no doubt feel I've gone overboard, especially my parents. But through the teachings of Maharishi I have become more aware of myself. . . . I have been able to reach deeper levels inside me. And there I have achieved a more relaxed state of mind—a serenity I have never before had. I know it's not for everyone, but it's right for me."

As she explained the concepts of TM, I found it a little hard to follow. I had heard before of the "mantra," a form of prayer or incantation. But she also used words like "prana," "kara," "bliss consciousness," and "creative intelligence." She said TM was not Hinduism, but it sounded very much like it to me. She talked about its founder, Maharishi Mahesh Yogi, how he had come to the United States in 1959 and was once a student of Guru Dev in India.

"It's hard to explain, I realize that," she said. "You really have to be there in the Ashram center to understand. But for the first time I feel at peace with myself. I never felt this way in my marriage. Sculpturing bridged the gap and helped me after the divorce. But there was no permanency there, either. But TM is different. It has helped me find God. Oh, by the way, this time next year I'll be in India. I plan to stay there a year or so visiting temples, great saints and teachers. I'm so excited about it. I have put my house up for sale. I hope it sells quickly. Real estate hasn't been moving too well lately, they tell me."

Her house did sell, and she did leave for India. But eight months after her departure, a cable arrived at my office. It read, "Coming home. Need to see you right away. Have breast lump. Barbara."

All arrangements were made. The afternoon of her scheduled admission to Memorial Hospital, I received a telephone call from Burt Thompson. Burt is a well-known Long Beach clinical psychologist and marriage counselor.

"Bob," he began, "I will be consulting on Barbara Fulton at the hospital later today. I understand she's having surgery tomorrow. Can you give me some background information?"

"Yes, Burt," I answered. "She has a large, fixed mass in her right breast along with some palpable lymph nodes under her right arm. She just got back from India. I had the surgeons see her two days ago. She is scheduled for a radical mastectomy tomorrow morning at 7:30. They feel the chance of its being malignant is extremely high—perhaps 95 percent."

I continued. "I'm glad you'll be seeing her, Burt. She was here in the office yesterday. She was really down. First time I've ever seen her that way. Del Hartman, the surgeon, was pretty frank with her. Kind of shook her up a bit when he presented all the facts. It doesn't look good, not good at all. By the way, did Del ask you to see her?"

"No. Actually, Barbara has been a client of mine for years – even before she and Don got divorced." Sensing my surprise, he said, "I know what you're thinking. Outwardly she appears to have it all together, doesn't she? Always so calm – like a rock. But inside it's been a struggle. This situation is going to really test her resources. It may be too much for her. But she has coped with trials in the past pretty well. I hope she'll be able to again. I'll do what I can."

"Burt, I'll call you after surgery tomorrow and give you the findings. Glad you're seeing Barbara. She's a great gal."

At about 5:00 that evening, I entered her hospital room. She was robed, lying in bed, turned toward the window. I was struck with how thin her arms and legs had become since the pilgrimage to India. Her chest wall heaved back and forth as she wept softly.

I touched her on the shoulder. She turned and looked up at me. Those eyes, always calm and serene, were entirely different now – helpless, pleading, filled with despair. Her face dropped into her hands as she cried out, "Oh my God, what's happening to me?"

Although my heart reached out to her, I was aware of another feeling within me. It was relief. At last this extraordinary person had been brought to a point of awareness, awareness of human limits, awareness of the need for help. Every person who is to receive new life must come to that point. I hoped this was the "preparatory event" God had chosen for her. I hoped this crisis would see her trading in the mantra for another prayer, a prayer in God's delivery room. And I hoped the surgeons would be wrong and the lump would be benign.

The next morning the surgeon's scissors were cutting through the fibrous and fatty tissues of the breast, freeing up a walnut-sized mass already attached to the anterior thoracic (chest) wall. The specimen was sent "stat" to the lab for an immediate report.

"Dr. Hartman," came the voice from the intercom, "this is Dr. Reinhold in Pathology. I have a frozen section report on a lesion from the right breast of Barbara Fulton. Am I in the correct room?"

After an affirmative answer, Dr. Reinhold went on, "The biopsy is malignant, repeat, it is malignant – an infiltrating intraductal carcinoma."

Dr. Hartman quietly and matter-of-factly turned to the nurse and said, "Let's begin the radical. Knife, please."

Doing It Our Way – Why It Thrives

Inside every person is a voice that says, "Get your needs satisfied!" We all respond in different ways. But there are really only two options, God's way or our way.

Barbara's husband, Don, went after prestige and achievement – getting ahead to fill the void. Barbara experimented with luxury living, then exchanged it for the world of art. Next came Eastern religion. I can't help but wonder what routes their children will choose growing up in the middle of such confusion.

Since the beginning of time, man, using his own "wisdom," has devised unlimited methods to find peace of mind. But it has all been a dismal failure, an utter waste of time. Though Barbara is now free, as far as I know, of the physical disease that had so frightened her, she has not yet found the avenue of real peace for her soul. The world's way has never brought us any closer to paradise, and common sense tells us it never will.

So why do we keep trying to do it our way over and over again? There are many reasons, but the most universal are pride and ego.

A prominent civic leader died recently. A good person, respected and admired for his unselfish devotion to the community, he loved people and people loved him. The newspaper headline read: "He Did It His Way."

That epitaph, meant to be strong and complimentary, in God's eyes was just the opposite. We can never do it our way and expect to please Him. He doesn't want the self-made man, the proud and boastful. As a matter of fact, the proud can never enter God's delivery room and find new life. It is not true that God helps those who help themselves. He helps those who *can't* help themselves. He wants the needy and humble. He "saves those who are *crushed in spirit*" (Psalm 34:18, emphasis added.

John C. Brizendine was a classic example of the great American success story. Several years ago, I read a front-page story about this exceptionally talented person. It told how he had risen to become president of Douglas Aircraft, a division of the huge McDonnell Douglas Corporation.

Brizendine had earned a reputation for community service as well as business innovation. He had many hobbies. His executive car had personalized plates, given to him by his wife, identifying *his* most famous product, the DC–10.

On May 25, 1979, Brizendine's comfortable world collapsed when an engine fell off an American Airlines DC–10 as it took off from Chicago's O'Hare International Airport. The plane plunged to earth, killing 273 people. Unbelievably, in the few months following the crash, two more DC–10s went down, one in Mexico City, another in Antarctica.

In the midst of all this, Brizendine and three other McDonnell Douglas officials were indicted for allegedly concealing payments to foreign airline agents in exchange for the purchase of their planes.

In just a matter of months, the life of this dynamic, self-sufficient businessman was changed from apparently glowing success to a life of worry and intense turmoil. After two years of endless legal haggling and negotiations, the charges were dropped. But the story of John Brizendine illustrates how quickly things can change. No one is exempt from crisis.

Another important reason why man ignores God and continues to choose his own formula for happiness is that *it does work*. There *is* pleasure in it—for a while. Diversions are successful, as long as life remains relatively tranquil. But crisis usually brings a quite different attitude. When doing it our way becomes a disaster, we begin to wonder if God's way might not be better.

Doing It Our Way and Crisis

A friend of mine tells how he was assigned to a refueling tanker carrying high octane gasoline throughout the Pacific during World War II. There wasn't a God-conscious cell in his body—until they started traveling through the mine fields of enemy waters. He then quickly developed an interest in spiritual matters.

Unable to find a Bible, he came across a book, *The Robe*, by Lloyd Douglas. It inspired him. "Lord," he prayed, "if you get me out of this, I promise to clean up my life. I'll change my whole way of living for You."

You see how differently we begin to think in the midst of a crisis? There are no atheists in fox-holes, as the old saying goes. Unfortunately, our deals with God are too often temporary.

Two weeks later my friend's ship pulled safe-
ly into port. He didn't forget his commitment—
for two or three hours, anyway—until the first bar,
the first girl, the first motel.

Lest you think it is always temporary,
however, let me finish the story. He did keep his
promise after all. Many years later this same man
entered God's delivery room. Today he does indeed live for the Lord.

Crisis and God's Delivery Room

A crisis is often the best method of revealing
the counterfeit nature of human paths to happiness. When it makes us aware of God's presence,
it actually becomes a blessing. Crisis may be the
loss of a loved one or a serious illness such as
cancer. Crisis can be personal defeat or the
dashing of a dream. Whatever form it takes, such
an unexpected trial is a divine shout beseeching
us to take a long, hard, reassessing look at our
priorities and philosophies. Crisis is designed to
tell us to *quit* doing it our way. If we're smart, we'll
listen.

Sometimes it takes a "sledgehammer" to get
our attention. Some of us have to reach the very
bottom before developing a hunger for spiritual
things. We must actually feel the mire of the pig
pen before recognizing God's sovereignty in our
lives.

God uses crises and problems to make His existence known. How patient He is with our stubbornness and resistance as we cling to our pride!

Fortunately, in the lives of those who do see and admit their need, God has already groomed them with certain preparatory events designed to bring them into His fold. There in His delivery room, they will ask Christ to enter their lives and to take over the controls. They will experience new birth and new life. They will be born again.

five

Christian or "Churchian?"

Only two of us were sitting in the operating room lounge that Saturday morning. Judy, the surgical scrub nurse, sat across the table from me, scanning the religion section of the newspaper. "What church do you go to, Judy?" I said.

"The Presbyterian," she said with a smile.

"Are you a Christian?" I asked.

Instantly her face showed total dismay. The puzzled expression spoke clearly, though without sound. I knew what she must be thinking: *Weren't you listening, Doctor? I just told you I was Presbyterian, and now you ask if I'm a Christian?*

She hid her true thoughts as she asked, "What do you mean, Doctor Wells?"

"Sounds like a dumb question I asked, Judy, but a lot of people think that going to church, belonging to a certain denomination, or living in the United States automatically makes them a Christian. That's no more true than going into a barn makes us a horse!"

She put down the newspaper, her expression registering an interest, so I was free to ask the next question. "What do you think a Christian is, Judy?"

"Well, I really never thought too much about it. I would say it's someone who believes in God *and* Jesus"—she quickly added the last—"and goes to church, and lives a good life—you know, the Golden Rule."

Her curiosity was aroused. Now it was her turn to ask, "What do you think a Christian is, Dr. Wells?"

"I guess we have to go back to the Bible to answer that question," I said. "The Bible says a Christian is one who has received new life."

"You mean being born again?" she responded. "My roommate has been talking to me about that. She says a person is not a Christian unless he is born again. Is that what you believe, Dr. Wells?"

"Yes, I do. The Bible says a Christian, a true believer, is one who has determined that Jesus Christ is exactly who He said He was, God in human flesh. Believing this fact by faith, that person then, at some point in time, invites Jesus

Christ into his or her life. A Christian is one in whom the Spirit of Christ lives."

"That seems so simple, doesn't it?"

"You bet it is, Judy. You see, Christianity does not mean worshipping a certain way. It has nothing to do with denominations. It doesn't make any difference if your hymnal is Methodist, Baptist or Lutheran. Whether you are Catholic or Protestant doesn't matter. True Christianity is not creeds, rituals or doctrine. How you take communion or your particular method of baptism is unimportant. Christianity is not a religion. It is an intimate and growing relationship with Jesus Christ."

During the next ten minutes, I shared with her about how God asks more of us than just believing in Him. We must believe also in His Son and then invite Jesus into our lives. I told her of the personal joy that comes to those who do. I knew her roommate would continue where I left off.

Judy's confusion about going to church and being a Christian is not unique. There are many people just like her who consider themselves Christians, yet they have never been in God's delivery room.

I call them "churchians." "Churchians" are *nonbelievers who go to church.* They are apparently unaware of the scriptural truth which says a child of God can only be *born* into the family. That means receiving, as a result of actually asking, Christ to be their Lord and Savior (John 1:12).

"Churchians" will say, "Yes, I believe in Jesus." But it's a pseudo-belief – they never act on it. Therefore, they never experience the new life of God's delivery room.

Simply believing the facts about Jesus Christ is not enough. Rather, a person must be so totally convinced by those facts that he is willing to turn over his whole life to Christ. That kind of belief is commitment – the critical ingredient for new spiritual life. Anything less produces "churchians," not Christians.

"Churchians" leave certain clues to their true nature and identity – not only in what they do, but especially in what they *don't* do. For example, people who belong to Christ will be producing at least some fruit. They will talk about Him, pray to Him, openly give Him credit and thanks for all things – as a habit of life. True Christians will be pulled to the Bible to learn more about Jesus. They will look for opportunities to share Christ with others as the Lord has commanded. These things are conspicuously absent in the life of a "churchian."

A "churchian" almost always finds the sanctuary where he feels least threatened. He prefers a minister who will soothe his conscience with cliches of comfort. He wants a place to "worship" that won't interfere with his life-style. The last thing he wants is the prick of conviction of guilt.

He gets nervous when the name of Jesus is mentioned. You can talk about God, but say the name Jesus and watch how fast the subject is changed. Some "churchians" become defensive. "Of course I'm a Christian," they say. "I go to church. You worship your way, and I'll worship mine. Religion is a personal thing." Many pews in America are occupied by pseudobelievers.

"Churchianity" is sad—sad because so many good, moral people have been situated too long in churches where traditions have been substituted subtly for God's Word. But the real tragedy is this: As long as "churchians" remain in the grip of a church devoid of Bible teaching, they never see the necessity of asking Christ into their lives. They travel along to the very end thinking they have salvation because they have church membership. A church can't save, of course—only Jesus can.

One patient, who I knew was attending a local church, had been coming to our office for her annual pap smears for ten years. From time to time she would describe the frustrations of a shaky marriage and the discouragement of dealing with a teenage son. On those occasions I would listen, then drop a thought or two from God's Word.

"Helen," I said to her once "just remember that 'unless the LORD builds the house, they labor in vain who build it' " (Psalm 127:1). As always, she was grateful and polite, but not interested.

I determined to be patient, content to wait for the right opportunity.

On her most recent visit, however, a change was evident. Always very attractive, that day she was radiant. Her eyes were alive, and she looked years younger. The smile that greeted me as I entered the examining room registered a major change.

"Hi, Dr. Wells," she said. "I feel just great. This has been the best year ever."

My eyes caught a small, gold fish pendant suspended from a chain around her neck. The fish encircled five familiar Greek letters: IXOYE.

"I see you know the King of kings," I said with a smile, pointing to the jeweled emblem.

"Oh, yes, Dr. Wells. I have some fantastic things to tell you. We finally made a decision to let *God* build our house."

For the next thirty minutes, Helen explained how she had been born again and what Christ had done for her marriage even for their rebellious teenager. It was good for her to tell it again, but she wouldn't have had to say a word. As soon as I saw the glow on her face, I knew she had invited Christ into her life. She had exchanged churchianity for Christianity.

six

Beginning a New Life

Physical life, remember, begins at conception. A tiny male seed penetrates the enclosing membrane of the female egg. This miraculous union, the fertilized egg, then grows in the uterus. Embryo becomes fetus, fetus becomes baby, and finally, nine months from the beginning, responding to the rhythmic contractions of labor, an infant makes its noisy debut. The setting for physical birth has traditionally been a room of tiled walls, sterile gowns, doctors, nurses and expectant parents waiting for the baby's first cry.

The goal of obstetrics is a healthy mother and child. Usually the baby's well-being can be predicted accurately in the delivery room from a small facial grimace. As the newborn's head emerges from the birth canal, a bulb syringe is gently inserted into the mouth to suction away secretions. If the tiny eyebrows knit together and the face winces as a reflex to this "intrusion," I am reassured that the baby is in good shape. There is no hurry. At that point I like to indulge in some light dialogue with the engrossed parents-to-be who are anxiously peering into the mirror.

Next the shoulders and arms of the infant are delivered, followed by buttocks and legs. I enjoy placing the baby immediately on the mother's abdomen, where some exciting events take place.

The baby will make a slight gasp, and then the little chest wall suddenly expands as air rushes in to fill the tiny air sacs. This full inspiration, the first breath, is quickly followed by a loud cry, the ultimate announcement that a new life has been created.

The infant is given to the nurse for some routine care but is soon right back in the arms of a proud and admiring mother. Still in the delivery room, the baby snuggles against mother's breast for a first taste of nourishment.

After allowing plenty of time for the child and parents to get acquainted, the child is finally transferred to the nursery, where he joins his "roommates" and soon begins crying along with them in almost perfect unison. More crying—another sign of health.

A bath has top priority in the nursery. This is carried out gently yet thoroughly by the nurse, who then wraps the newborn in warm blankets and places him or her in an open plastic crib alongside the observation window. Jubilant family and friends peer through that window. I think they all use the same script: "He's so cute." "Just look at those tiny fingers." "He looks just like his father." "Oh, I can't wait to hold her."

But the line I like best is, "He's bald like Grandpa!" Grandpas, however don't appreciate that one much.

And in the nursery, the baby even begins to grow.

Spiritual life also begins at "conception." It occurs the instant the "seed" so persuades an individual that he is able to believe it by faith. The seed is of course the gospel message – that Christ, the Son of God, died for us that we might have eternal life.

But spiritual conception is just the first step toward this new life offered by God. Believing must be accompanied by action. There must be a birth experience – one that comes later in God's delivery room. The obstetrical suite of this birth is quite unique, for it is not located just in a hospital. Rather, it can be anywhere, for it is the place, the exact site, where every Christian-elect prays to receive Christ as Lord and Savior. This is where God hears the cry of His newborn child.

God's Delivery Room

Each new Christian will experience the same sequence of events that occurs in the hospital delivery room. There in His delivery room God sees His newborn "grimace" as that person realizes his one great need that can be met only when pride and ego are brushed aside. That is painful! Generally, the bigger the ego, the bigger the grimace.

The next crucial event for the newborn Christian is receiving the breath of life. Just as God created Adam by breathing into him (Genesis 2:7), so He also breathes spiritual life into every new believer (John 20:22). No one has ever been born again without this all-important infusion.

This miracle of being filled with the Holy Spirit is immediately followed by the baby's "cry." This cry is our only required action. It is our prayer. It admits our sin and our need for help. It is a prayer of invitation: "Jesus, come into my life."

But being a child of God brings with it definite responsibilities that will quickly test the depth of our commitment. They begin in the "nursery."

GOD'S NURSERY

Confessing

The crying that continues in the nursery is the equivalent of proclaiming, or confessing, our new relationship with God. Our Lord wants and expects us to cry out. He doesn't want secret-service disciples. He wants bold servants. And so He commands us to tell others about our new life.

Everyone therefore who shall confess Me before men, I will also confess him before My Father who is in heaven (Matthew 10:32).

If you confess with your mouth Jesus as Lord, and believe in your heart that God raised Him from the dead, you shall be saved (Romans 10:9).

Whoever confesses that Jesus is the Son of God, God abides in him, and he in God (1 John 4:15).

A willingness to be identified publicly with Jesus Christ is solid evidence that our commitment is from the heart, not just from the head. "Going public" tests and strengthens our decision. Because of this, many churches provide an opportunity to go forward (altar call) at the end of a service to affirm our new life in Christ.

The audience with whom we share our delivery room experience need not be large. For those who are somewhat reserved or perhaps uneasy in front of people, a family member or friend is quorum enough. The main thing is to tell *someone*.

Confessing our Christianity is somewhat like taking a wedding vow. Before the wedding ceremony, we can have strong emotional and intellectual ties with our betrothed. But there is no legal relationship until the vows have been taken. Two people are married *only* after they have stood before witnesses and verbally committed themselves to each other. A meaningful "marriage" to Christ, though sealed with a personal commitment to Him as Savior, is solidified with a *public* acknowledgment.

Baptism

Just as the bath in the nursery has top priority for each newborn, so God also gives it top priority for His "newborns." He asks that we begin our new life by being baptized. Mark 16:16 says, "He who has believed and has been baptized shall be saved." Our baptism affirms that we are neither fearful nor ashamed of our decision. It also provides an excellent opportunity to give witness of our new faith to others.

Growing

The third responsibility of each Christian is to grow spiritually (2 Peter 3:18). Spiritual growth is the gradual process by which God molds us into the kind of people He wants us to be. It is the very essence of our new life.

The key to this kind of growth is a wholesome and well-balanced spiritual diet. That is why in God's delivery room and nursery the newborn is given milk right away. "Like newborn babes, long for the pure milk of the word, that by it you may grow in respect to salvation" (1 Peter 2:2). The new Christian who "snuggles" closer to God's Word is on the right track.

Nancy, a patient of mine, is an excellent example of how important our spiritual diet can be. One evening while walking past the Women's Hospital lobby, I spotted her.

"Hi, Doctor Wells," she said. "Her smile was

not at full power.

"Well hi, Nancy," I responded. "What brings you here?"

"My brother's wife just had a baby, and I was waiting to see her during visiting hours."

I could see Nancy was preoccupied, worried. So I asked, "Is there anything wrong? You look a bit on the down side."

"Doctor Wells," she replied, "could I speak to you a minute?"

"Sure. I'm done with rounds. We can talk in the family room. It's right over here."

In the small room this young housewife and mother poured out her heart. Bouts of depression had become more frequent and intense the last few years, including even suicidal thoughts. The neurologist to whom she was referred had ruled out any organic cause for her despondency. He felt her symptoms were probably the result of increased tensions and responsibilities.

"These times of depression are frightening, Doctor Wells. I've even been to a psychologist, but that didn't help. I didn't tell you back then, but after our baby was born, I really became depressed. It wasn't just the baby blues. It was worse, much deeper than that. It took months to get over the severe phase. I even went back to teaching just to get my mind off myself and my problems. I'm not sure that was the right thing to do, because then I found myself enjoying work more than taking care of Becky. And that brought guilt. I felt so ashamed, like I was a failure as a mother. Becky is four now. Can you believe it? And such a good little girl.

"Then two years ago I began having terrible phobias, like being afraid of heights and closed-in places. I couldn't go anywhere if it meant flying or going across high bridges. I even had to avoid elevators and crowded department stores. That was when I started seeing a psychologist."

"What about your husband?" I asked.

"Oh, Tom has been super. He is the most understanding husband in the whole world. I know he is very concerned about me. I've been such a strain on him.

"Doctor Wells, I know you're a Christian and so you'll understand what I'm going to say. Last year we started attending church. Six months ago both Tom and I asked Jesus to come into our lives. I thought all my emotional problems would be solved. But I'm still a mess. I just can't seem to cope with things, and I'm really scared. Tom thinks having another baby is what we need, but I'm afraid the depression will start all over and be even worse. I'm sorry to burden you with all my troubles, but I just don't know what to do."

"Well, Nancy, I can tell you one thing. You did the right thing by asking God to come in and take over. However, becoming a Christian doesn't mean instant cure. Neither does it bring a trouble-free life. As a friend of mine said recently, 'It's not a day at Disneyland with a pocket full of "E" tickets.' "

She laughed, and I continued. "Sometimes, after becoming a Christian, things get worse, and I believe that's the way it's supposed to be. I'll tell you why.

"A long time ago, I felt exactly the same way you do. When I surveyed my own situation, it was obvious I was actually having more problems as a Christian than I had had before. Some of them were pretty heavy. I kept asking myself why.

"The answer is simple. When we become a child of God, His one desire is for us to grow. How it must hurt Him when we remain in diapers long after our new birth. The fact is that spiritual maturity simply will not take place when things are going smoothly. It is during those times that we tend to rely on our own strengths and not on God. Pride creeps in, and that's not good. The Lord never wants us reading our own press clippings. He wants us to depend solely on Him, 100 percent! And since He is the one in charge of all circumstances, He will allow difficult situations in our lives for a definite purpose. He wants us to develop a lifetime habit of trusting in Him for everything."

"I sure wish there were an easier way of growing," Nancy said. "Don't you, Dr. Wells?"

"And how," I replied. "Growing up spiritually is a painful process. But it's worth it. The more mature we are, the more meaningful life becomes."

I asked a few questions. The first one gave her the opportunity to tell how she and Tom came to receive Christ as their Savior. Their spiritual experience seemed genuine. Then I asked what she had been doing since that commitment. It was what she had *not* been doing that held the key.

"Come on, Nancy. Let's go over to the nursery," I said. I decided the best counsel would be visual.

We stood together in front of the viewing window. A sign above read "Growing Nursery." Inside, a nurse was in the process of putting her hand and arm through the small porthole of an isolette to feed formula to a scrawny, premature baby.

"See that bottle, Nancy? What's in it?"

"Milk," she replied.

"Right. Without milk that baby would not make it out of the premature class. Its lack of growth would then alert the pediatrician, who would soon make the diagnosis of 'failure to thrive.' Next he would have to find out why. One of the most common reasons for this condition is poor nutrition. Now, Nancy, let me ask you. Are you growing spiritually at a steady rate, or are you failing to thrive?"

"For sure, I'm not doing so hot in the growth department. Lately I've even wondered if I really am a Christian since I still haven't got my act together."

Nancy was a baby Christian suffering from malnutrition.

I went on. "Nancy, in the milk the nurse is feeding that 'premie' are the three essential foodstuffs: fat, protein, and carbohydrate. If one or more of these ingredients is left out of a child's diet, it will always be malnourished. This leads to stunting of growth and susceptibility to disease.

"In the same way, every Christian needs three important spiritual foodstuffs in his diet. They are daily prayer, daily Bible study, and Christian fellowship. They are critically important to maintaining good spiritual health."

I glanced at my watch. "Hey, I'm keeping you from seeing your sister-in-law."

"No, please go on, Dr. Wells. I need to hear this."

"Well, the first spiritual food we need is daily prayer. We can see that in Philippians 4:6. You and I are members of God's family. He is our Father, and like all good fathers He wants time alone with His child. Prayer really is just communicating, and communicating is how two people get to know one another.

"But prayer is more than that, Nancy. Prayer is the most important power tool we can have in our workshop. Nothing has impressed me more as a Christian than what prayer can accomplish.

It is absolutely amazing. Our problem is that we either forget to use it or we avoid it assuming it won't work. But there is real power in prayer.

"Reading the Bible each day is equally as important. God wants us to be like His Son, to think, act, and respond as Jesus would. That means we must read as much about Him as we can.

"Reading His Word regularly also helps us to stay away from sin, as we see in Psalm 119:11. And that is a battle we all fight.

"And the last indispensable ingredient is regular church attendance and Christian fellowship, as we read in Hebrews 10:25. Without it we will invariably stray and begin to walk with the world again—the very same one we left when we found God. Every one of us needs the encouragement of fellow believers to keep our Christian walk straight.

"I remember when I finally stopped allowing other priorities like golf and racquetball to interfere with Sunday church. Shortly thereafter I experienced a most welcome growth spurt."

I continued. "From personal experience, I can tell you that whenever I feel far away from God, I am also far away from those proper foods. As one very close friend of mine has said, 'If I omit them for even one day, I know something is wrong. If I leave them out two days, *my wife* knows something is wrong. If I leave them out for a week or more, *everyone* knows something is wrong!'

"Nancy, what you are telling me is that there is a problem with growth in your life. So let me ask you what your own spiritual diet has been like since becoming a Christian."

She looked over at me and without the slightest hesitation said, "I've been starving!"

I took her by the arm. "Now let me show you still another nursery."

We walked down the hallway to Children's Hospital. I stopped in front of the window marked "Intensive Care Nursery." It was a full house. Every isolette held a sick infant fighting for its life. Nurses, IVs, tubes, monitors, sophisticated machines, and computers surrounded the world of each tiny creature.

"Here is the other cause of 'failure to thrive,' " I said. "It is disease. The offending disease is often chronic and usually serious. Again, growth is markedly affected."

Seeing her smile I continued, "You guessed correctly, Nancy. There are also spiritual diseases that can attack newborn Christians. They are usually subtle and insidious. These diseases are such things as giving priority to material things new cars, fancy homes, expensive vacations. It is easy to get sucked back into the life of self-pleasure, career, and climbing the social ladder. These things invariably inhibit our growth and do it so cunningly that sometimes the diagnosis of 'failure to thrive' is made too late.

"There is nothing wrong with having nice things... unless they come between us and God. They become idols of worship. Then, we must get them out as fast as we can, or they will destroy us spiritually."

Nancy and I talked longer. We found several "dietary deficiencies" and "disease processes" that were adversely influencing her Christian growth. She seemed comforted to know that all Christians fight the same ongoing battle against spiritual malnutrition and chronic disease. I know I sure do!

Since that evening, I am happy to tell you that Nancy's walk with God has improved dramatically. The episodes of depression that torment her come far less frequently. Phobias? They're gone. Trusting God is the prescription for fear. Oh yes, she also had another baby, and without any post-partum blues.

In this new life of ours, we are expected to "grow in the grace and knowledge of our Lord and Savior Jesus Christ" (2 Peter 3:18). In fact, spiritual growth is what Christian living is all about. But it can happen only when we follow God's specific dietary recommendation – daily Bible, daily prayer, and regular fellowship with other believers. The amount of growth is going to be directly proportional to the time spent in these vital areas.

seven

Infertility and Reproductive Failure

Infertility is a gynecological term that refers to difficulty in conceiving. Reproductive failure, on the other hand, is an obstetrical term. It refers to any condition occurring in pregnancy (e.g., miscarriage), that prevents live, viable birth. Both of these classifications can also be used in a spiritual way.

Spiritual Infertility

"And some were being persuaded by the things spoken, but others would not believe" (Acts 28:24).

If the gospel "seed" fails to penetrate the heart of a person, there will be no "conception" and, of course, no born-again experience. The listening party may be unable to believe or perhaps just unwilling to believe.

Melvin Dunning illustrates someone who simply could not believe. The rise of this man to financial prominence was well known in the community. At forty-two he became president and chairman of the board of a large savings and loan company. At age forty-eight he was worth a fortune. His five thousand-square-foot home was featured in an article in *Better Homes and Gardens*. He owned about every luxury item available to man. He worked hard, he played hard. But the result of it all was coronary problems.

The evening before his scheduled open heart surgery, he and his close friend and golf companion, Greg Hanson, were talking together. Greg was a real estate broker. He, too, was financially well off. But his priorities were quite different from Mel's. Greg was a Christian. For eleven years he had talked about the gospel story with his friend. But Mel's response was always the same, just as on the night of this conversation.

"Mel, would you mind if I prayed with you before I leave?" Greg asked.

"I'd like that, Greg. I'd like that very much."

Greg Hanson's prayer revealed the deep affection and concern he felt for his dear friend who would be wheeled into the operating room for a coronary bypass the next morning.

When the prayer was finished, Mel spoke. "Greg, I wish I could believe as you do. I really do. But I can't. But don't worry about me, good buddy, we'll be on the course in six weeks. That's a promise!"

Mel did not keep that promise. In fact, the two of them never again played golf together. In the recovery room, immediately following an eight hour operation, a blood clot found its way to Mel's brain—a massive stroke. For three days Mel remained in a coma, and on the fourth day he died.

Greg was heartbroken. The day of the funeral, Greg vented his frustration to me as we talked together at the cemetery.

"Why, Bob? Why do some people continue to resist God's plan for their lives? I'll never understand it. Never."

Tears were in his eyes as he told me the obvious. He would never see his friend again, neither here on earth nor in heaven.

Mel wanted to believe, but he couldn't. Another person I know doesn't even want to believe. This man is in his late seventies. It seems he had never forgiven God for allowing his grandson to be born with a physical deformity. He had been unable to reconcile a God of love allowing such a thing to happen. So he wants nothing to do with Him.

This man knows what the gospel says. A concerned friend once gave him an excellent book, written by Billy Graham, clearly presenting the message of salvation. When he finished reading the book and returned it, his only comment was, "I disagree." He had made it clear. He wanted nothing to do with God, for God had done him an "injustice."

Other Reasons for Spiritual Infertility

There are many reasons people reject the gospel message. Let's examine some others.

1. *Not logical.* Doctors are excellent examples of those in the intellectual arena who reject Jesus Christ because the gospel is, in their minds, not logical. For members of the medical community, faith is particularly elusive—it goes against the grain of scientific reasoning.

Every physician is trained in medical school, internship and residency to believe only what is seen or can be explained rationally. There is no room for conjecture or "faith." Something is real only if we taste it, see it, smell it, hear it or feel it.

The problem is obvious. God has asked each human being to believe by faith that there is eternal life, although we have never seen it. He asks that we believe Christ died on the cross for us, although we have never seen Him. That confounds the doctor. He considers it intellectual suicide to choose faith as a basis for his philosophy of life.

Yet physicians use faith every day. They have faith that the drugs they order are not contaminated. They have faith that the equipment they use in surgery is safe. They have faith that the brakes and steering wheels of their cars will always respond. But when it comes to the major issue of life itself, faith suddenly has no role. The percentage of physicians who are Christians is low.

One doctor recently did shed pride and ego, and just in time. He was an extremely busy and energetic physician, but his whirlwind life-style took its toll. One day he was stricken with a near-fatal heart attack.

A friend came to the hospital and gave him the gospel message. The doctor recognized his own need and understood and believed what he heard. There in his hospital room, with his friend, he asked Christ to come into his life. That hospital room was the delivery room God had picked for him.

During the next few weeks, while convalescing at home, he not only read the Bible with unquenchable thirst, but also discussed its truths with many. As it turned out, his lifetime was limited, but it was spent with purpose serving his Lord.

2. *Improper priorities.* The next obstacle keeping people from receiving Christ is improper priorities. Moses certainly understood the problem when he cautioned, "If you ever forget the LORD your God, and go after other gods and serve them and worship them, I testify against you today that you shall surely perish" (Deuteronomy 8:19).

Business, travel, finances, and social life remain on top of the priority list for many people. Those are their "gods," the idols they worship. Their busy schedules leave no time for Jehovah

God. The Lord knew this when He said, "Where your treasure is, there will your heart be also" (Matthew 6:21). For this group, the pull of those "treasures" is just too great.

An ambitious vice-president of a large corporation, a driving, energetic business woman and a money-minded dentist are all held hostage by material possessions and recognition. But these three individuals all have another thing in common. On a shelf in each of their homes is a book, and in that book it says, "For what does it profit a man to gain the whole world, and forfeit his soul?" (Mark 8:36).

3. *The price is too high.* Many say, "No, thank you," because of an unwillingness to relinquish a style of living. I know some who appear addicted to country club life, cocktail parties and "horsing around." They call it the "good life." They shun Christianity for fear of what others may say. The last thing they want is to be labeled a religious nut.

Others resist because of what they think must be given up. How wrong they are! God does not demand that we give up anything except control over our lives. The Bible does not say that to have eternal life we must give up gambling, swearing, smoking, drinking and dancing.

Christianity is not a religion of don'ts. In fact, it isn't a religion at all. It is a personal relationship with a living God. And it is this same God who tells us not to worry about those habits. He promises to clean up our lives in such a way that we'll never miss any of our sinful pleasures.

4. *I'm not worthy — yet.* I recall a person's telling me in my backyard one day, "I have never made a commitment because I'm not yet worthy. I believe God expects me first to get my life together, to make it more presentable. Only then would I ever feel right asking Him into my life."

That kind of reasoning is sincere, but it is sincerely wrong. "God demonstrates His own love toward us, in that while we were yet sinners, Christ died for us" (Romans 5:8).

It's great to know that God takes us just the way we are. He reserves for Himself the job of remodeling our lives.

5. *No need.* Some people seem not to sense a need. A physician friend is a nonbeliever. He has a wonderful wife and a loving relationship with her, and he has beautiful children. His family appears happy in every way. They take many vacations and are blessed with all the comforts.

He lives a moral life. He is kind and thoughtful, and he enjoys his work. Everything seems to run smoothly. Oh, there may be a few problems with relatives, but in general, disruptions in their day-to-day living are rare.

Has he ever "grimaced" from need? Not so far. His life has never been interrupted with financial reverses, illness or death in the family. Maybe he has a need but he has not yet recognized it. I wonder if the person who was last heard on the American Airlines Flight 191 in-flight recorder crying out, "Oh my God!" had felt a need just minutes before when the ill-fated DC–10 taxied onto the Chicago runway for what everyone expected to be a routine take-off. Any one of us could have our lives snuffed out abruptly without a moment's notice. "Need" often comes unannounced.

6. *I've always believed.* Some folks assume they are Christians because of their parents. But being raised in a Christian home does not exempt anybody from personally needing to enter God's delivery room. There are no automatic Christians; God has no grandchildren. He has only children, those who at a specific point in time have prayed to receive Christ (John 1:12).

7. *Turned off by Christians.* Unfortunately, many people hold back because of weaknesses and inconsistencies in the lives of professed Christians. "He's just a hypocrite!" they say. And they may well be right. People forget that Christians are human beings, too. They struggle like everyone else.

I can't speak for other churches, but I suspect they are just like ours. Our church is a hospital. We have "sick" folks there. We have problems and are subject to the same pressures and temptations as everyone else. The bumper sticker seen around town best explains this principle: "Christians aren't perfect, just forgiven."

If someone says no to God because of what he sees in the lives of Christians, he is looking at the wrong example. *Christianity means looking at Christ, not people.* If you look at man, you'll be disappointed every time.

8. *Aging.* Aging brings with it a resistance to spiritual matters. The longer we live, the more stubborn and set in our ways we become. As the twilight years approach, the heart becomes harder and more insensitive.

But for those senior citizens who enter the Lord's delivery room, the reward is just the same, just as meaningful and just as satisfying as for their younger counterparts.

9. *Pride, ego, and wealth.* These obstacles represent the lion's share of those who refuse to respond to the knock on the door. Interestingly, too, those obstacles usually go together.

A man I know, getting along in years, is the pillar of his community – strong, self-reliant, resourceful, talented. Considered by all, including himself, to be self-made, he had enjoyed great monetary success.

His church attendance is impeccable, but his philosophy of life does not come from the Bible. To my knowledge, he has never given God credit for his long list of achievements. His conversation remains self-centered and self-edifying. Can he not see that it was God who gave him the personality, good mind and good health to succeed?

Scripture deals with this issue: "You may say in your heart, 'My power and the strength of my hand made me this wealth.' But you shall remember the LORD your God, for it is He who is giving you power to make wealth" (Deuteronomy 8:17–18).

It is God who has given us everything we have, and He can take it all away just as He gave it. When tragedy strikes and the rich and proud stand naked before the Lord, perhaps with illness, cancer, a broken marriage, grief or material reversal, they can be thankful that Christ's death on the cross was for *everyone,* rich and poor alike. God's merciful hand will still reach out to them as He says, "Please enter My delivery room, but first leave your pride and ego in the lobby."

Spiritual Reproductive Failure – Miscarriage

In Matthew 13, Jesus described what amounts to spiritual miscarriage in His parable of the soils. Parables are earthly stories with heavenly meanings. Therefore, in this particular parable, each soil represents an individual hearing the gospel and the impact it has on his life.

All four people in the story heard the same message. Of the four, however, only the last to hear truly understood. Only this one became born again and produced fruit.

Why? What was different about the other three? They each heard and they each responded. So why did they miscarry? The answer is that they failed to understand in their hearts the full meaning of the message. Their heads understood, but their hearts did not.

The first listener (soil) heard about the power of Jesus Christ, and he responded in a positive way. But the response was weak and without commitment. Almost immediately the world pulled him away and substituted something else in its place.

The second hearer (soil) heard the gospel of Jesus with joy. But again the bond was either not right or fetal nourishment was inadequate, for the person quickly abandoned his "faith" when confronted with temptations or personal problems.

One of my patients illustrates this second soil. Her happiness and excitement were clearly evident when she first heard what Jesus Christ could do for her. One Sunday her family witnessed with delight her public declaration of faith. She began to attend church regularly and even a home Bible study, but she soon dropped out. She also resisted baptism, another clue something was amiss.

Now the Bible and church are no longer a part of her. There has been no outward change in her life. She is still lonely, self-centered and lazy, and she continues a live-in relationship with her boyfriend. Today lawyers call it cohabitation; God calls it fornication.

Her refusal to seek a life-style pleasing to God seems to indicate her delivery room prayer was a sham. She needs to get on her knees and ask

Jesus Christ into her life—*and mean it.*

The parable's third person (soil) hearing the gospel of Jesus Christ was also touched and moved. However, preoccupation with worldly things interfered with the nourishment every new Christian must have in the "womb." He aborted somewhere along the way, never reaching the Lord's delivery room.

A professional man I know has a spiritual story that parallels this soil. He had described to others how he asked Christ into his life one day while watching a religious TV broadcast. But like many others, his heart must not have understood, because many years have now gone by and, although he occasionally attends church, outwardly he is absolutely no different from the way he was before his "conversion."

His priorities tell the story. Since his professed delivery room experience, he remains wrapped up in social activities, job and investments. His busy world has no time for Bible, prayer, church or Christian fellowship. To put it bluntly, he has given God the scraps.

Something happened to him shortly after conception. Those false gods of materialism, career, personal pleasures and recognition kept this man from receiving the Lord's intrauterine feedings. Although he has the potential to be a giant servant and testimony for the Lord, he seems willing to trade it all away for the cramping pain of spiritual miscarriage.

In summary, then, the "good news" about Jesus Christ was heard by all four people in the parable, yet only one, the fourth listener, understood down deep inside where it counts. Only that person "completed the journey down the (Fallopian) tube and into the cavity of the uterus."

Spiritual birth hinges on two things. First, the full significance of what Christ has done for each of us — i.e., the gospel — must be fully understood. Second, our acceptance of His great gift must be genuine. It must be a commitment from the heart. Absence of either or both of these requisites spells miscarriage every time.

eight

A Family Concern

I had just gone to sleep when the telephone rang. It was 11 P.M.

"Bob, you'd better get over here right away," I heard my father say when I picked up the phone. "Your mom is sick. It looks bad."

"I'll be right there, Dad."

Five minutes later I was at my mother's bedside. She was having chest pains and had no detectable blood pressure. Pale and weak, she cried out pitifully for help. The pain was unbearable. There could be only one explanation, a massive heart attack. The paramedics arrived immediately.

At the hospital our family prayed together just a few feet from the treatment room where the cardiac team was working diligently. Then two physicians stepped into the doorway of the family room. Before they spoke, we knew Mom had died. The woman we loved so much was gone.

Despite all the valiant attempts at home and in the emergency room to revive this precious woman, her oxygen-deprived heart had stopped.

During the difficult days and weeks that followed, we never doubted Mom was with the Lord. At the age of fourteen, she had received Jesus Christ as her Savior. Her remaining sixty-one years confirmed that commitment. Earlier, while her health was good, Mom had made it a point to tell us about her born-again experience. And we're so glad she did.

"God has given us eternal life, and this life is in His Son. He who has the Son has the life; he who does not have the Son of God does not have the life" (1 John 5:11, 12). Those verses gave us much comfort as we faced the reality that Mom would no longer be a part of our lives on earth. She now lives with Jesus. My mother cannot come to us, but we can *and will* go to her.

Biblical truths can sometimes be agony for the Christian as he relates to loved ones. He knows only too well how Scripture describes the consequences of outright rejection of God's message. "Those who do not wish to know God, and who refused to accept His plan to save them through our Lord Jesus Christ ... will be punished in everlasting hell, forever separated from the Lord" (2 Thessalonians 1:8, 9, TLB).

It is little wonder that Christians so

desperately want to know how each member of their family stands with the Lord. God doesn't want Christians to go to heaven alone.

Silent Believers

In the family of most Christians is at least one silent believer, often of an older generation. He is one who simply believes in Jesus Christ as Savior but has not felt the need to declare that commitment to others. At some time in his life, he made a definite decision to trust in Jesus Christ. Probably someone else does know about it. However, since that revelation it has been held in secret, leaving his Christian family members entirely in the dark – wondering, always wondering.

Jesus Himself emphasized the importance of telling others about our faith. "Everyone therefore who shall confess Me before men, I will also confess him before My Father who is in heaven" (Matthew 10:32). Romans 10:9 states clearly that we must not only believe in our heart that Jesus Christ is God, but also confess that belief openly to others.

Becoming a genuine Christian, then, is twofold. First, we must believe. The silent believer has done this. Second, it should have such an impact on us that we are compelled to tell others about it. Here the silent believer has been lacking.

If you have been stingy in your witness, now is the time to tell your family about your having received Christ into your life. If you don't, Christian members of your family left behind, possibly even your own spouse, may spend a lifetime wondering if you ever said the most important words anyone can say, "Jesus, I believe—and receive." There is no greater comfort to a Christian than to know that each member of his family has received eternal life.

I'll never forget the evening my dad and I talked over dessert at Polly's Pies Restaurant. He told me every detail of his delivery room experience. At age fifteen, he walked forward in church to affirm his commitment to Christ.

Dad's life alone seemed ample evidence that he was a child of God, but what a thrill it was for me to hear it firsthand. I didn't really need the pie and ice cream that night, but I sure needed what Dad said to me.

Perhaps you can now understand why some of your own family may seem so curious to know where you stand spiritually. You may think they are overly zealous, even pushy. But their motive, quite likely, is pure love.

"I would even give my own life if Mom and Dad could just know the Lord the way I do." Those were the words of a nineteen-year-old Christian college student who had just that kind of love for his parents. Several months later God granted that wish.

One Saturday morning in our kitchen, Brad,

who was spending the weekend with us, was discussing his goals. This very bright young man from Michigan wanted to be a doctor. His mind was sharp, his manner was personable; he cared. *He would be a fine physician,* I thought to myself. He asked about my specialty.

"OB is a very satisfying field, Brad," I said, "but the night work is the pits."

Brad thought for a minute, then said, "You're right. Maybe I'd better be a dermatologist."

He and my wife had several meaningful conversations in our kitchen. Brad discussed how much he missed his parents and his deep, abiding desire to see them become Christians. My wife seemed always to have just the right words for him.

Two weeks after his last visit to our home, Brad collapsed in his dormitory room. The entire right side of his body was paralyzed, and he remained unconscious. A congenital defect in a major blood vessel of the brain had ruptured, and the hemorrhage had left in its wake extensive and irreparable cerebral damage.

While Brad lay comatose in the hospital, his father stayed at the college. Brad's mother remained in Michigan, immobilized by shock and grief.

During the next eight days, Brad's classmates poured out their love to his father. Thousands of students presented their prayers to God. Wooed by this unity of spirit and trust in the Lord, Brad's father chose to enter God's delivery room, receiving Jesus Christ as his Lord and Savior just two days before his son died. Later we heard that two weeks after Brad's death, his mother, still in Michigan, also had turned her life over to Jesus.

My wife wrote the young man's mother and described some of the warm talks she and their son had enjoyed at our breakfast table. In her words, "Brad is now in the presence of the Lord. God has called him for something more important than what he had on earth."

Brad's prayers were answered. His parents did come to know Jesus Christ. But it seemed to take his own homegoing to bring them to spiritual birth. To all who knew this fine student, his death seemed a tragedy. But perhaps it was God's way of bringing two more (and possibly others we don't know about) to His delivery room.

"My faith is a personal matter between me and God." Have you, silent believer, ever said that to someone? Christians in your family are starving to know if you have Christ in your life. They may be afraid to ask for fear of upsetting you, but you can be sure they want to know.

Your faith is *not* just between you and God. It is an issue of utmost importance to every believer who loves you. Imagine the agony they may be feeling this very moment, wondering if they will ever see you again—in heaven.

Don't assume that because you are a good person and live an unselfish life, everyone will know you are a Christian. Lots of people live good lives, but that doesn't necessarily mean they are Christians.

One patient described the time she confronted her own father about his relationship with God. He had leukemia, and the prognosis was not good. She wrestled for a long time about how to approach the subject. Finally she decided to ask him right out. "Dad, are you a Christian?" she asked one night in the hospital.

Her father was flabbergasted. "Haven't I lived a life that answers that question?" he blurted out.

"I think so, Dad, but real Christianity is not only how we live, but also what we believe."

"Well, I've always believed in God," he said.

"Dad, a lot of people believe in God. The Bible says even the demons believe in God. Christianity hinges on whether we believe in His Son. What I need to know, Pop, is whether you have ever asked Jesus Christ into your life."

The young woman and her father came closer together that evening than ever before. It was a time of great joy as they hugged and wept openly, and he told her every detail surrounding his entry into the Lord's delivery room. He *had* believed in Jesus Christ and received Him as Savior. The problem was that he had simply neglected to tell his own family.

Tell your family now, silent believer. Tell your family all the details of your own delivery room. Don't place your loved ones in the uneasy position of having to ask you. *Tell them.*

A word to the *unbeliever:* What greater expression of love could you give to those Christians around you than at least to look at God's proposition? Examine the facts about Jesus. Then decide for yourself. If you still don't believe, explain why to your family. At least you will have taken the time to explore the greatest of all life's issues.

nine

Why Me?

The question most often asked during a crisis is "Why me?" One of the great rewards of our new birth is the luxury of finally being able to answer that question. "And we know that all that happens to us is working for our good if we love God and are fitting into his plans" (Romans 8:28, TLB). That is God's great promise to His children.

What this verse tells us is that *all* things that enter our lives (including the unwelcome) are working for our good. That is a fantastic promise when you stop to think about it. It means pain, suffering, trials, disappointments – all the things we fear the most – are there for a reason, which is *our* good. It is guaranteed in writing by God Himself.

New birth corrects our humanistic myopia and allows us to finally see things from God's perspective, not just our own. Once we understand that the Lord is in total control of every situation and every circumstance, we have the resource to accept adversity with confidence rather than with indignation and discouragement.

All that sounds good. But does it work in reality? Some years ago I was delivering Melinda's baby. In those days, husbands were not yet being allowed in the delivery room. Her prenatal course and labor were normal, and I was anticipating no problems. I was wrong.

As the baby eased into my gloved hands, I could hear the familiar background sounds of the delivery room stop abruptly. This time there would be no "He's so beautiful!" from the attending nurses. As I held the baby in my lap and suctioned out the mouth, my eyes quickly scanned the newborn.

Every classic sign of Down's syndrome (formerly called mongolism) was present. My heart sank as I saw the typical, broad, mongoloid appearance with its characteristic vertical fold of skin just inside each eye. Running across each of the baby's palms was a single transverse crease. The fingers were stubby, and the fifth digit on each hand was inappropriately short.

Melinda sensed from the silence that something was wrong. "Dr. Wells, is my baby okay?" she asked.

Life in the delivery room is not always pleasant. Only obstetricians know the haunting anxiety accompanying moments like that. No matter how carefully the answer to such a question is worded, it never seems quite right. Invariably it leaves you with an empty feeling, a feeling of failure for not having communicated it in a better way. That question, "Is the baby all right?" can be a nightmare.

Melinda was a nurse, and I knew she would understand the term I had to use next.

"Melinda, it is a boy, but we have a problem. He appears to have Down's syndrome. The pediatrician is on his way right now to check the baby over, but I'm pretty sure he will agree."

Even before I finished the sentence, I knew I had been too blunt. *Oh Lord,* I thought to myself, *isn't there a better way than this? I feel so helpless.*

I clamped and cut the baby's cord and handed the pathetic little child to the pediatrician, who had just arrived. After the examination, his nod told me the diagnosis was correct. The pediatrician then went over to the delivery table to explain the situation to the devastated new mother, who was then being comforted by one of the nurses. I finished sewing up the episiotomy.

Melinda was sobbing uncontrollably. "No, no, no. Why me, why me?"

I waited a few moments, then said, "Melinda, we'll have a chance to talk more about things later. Right now I'll tell Bill, and then you and he can spend as much time together as you need in the recovery room. Okay?" I knew there would be no answer.

Melinda's husband was standing in the doorway of the fathers' waiting room when I walked up still in my scrub suit. I had become acquainted with Bill earlier while Melinda labored. He had just graduated from college that week. What a great graduation gift this was going to be, he had commented.

He had worked hard for his degree, carrying seventeen units a semester and still holding down a full-time job. It was with more than a hint of pride that he showed me his new class graduation ring with its black onyx stone encircled by the university's letters.

I had been very impressed with Bill's sharp mind and humor. And he was certainly very handsome, as all the nurses at the core station remarked. He was excited in the labor room and did not hesitate to voice his preference for a son.

As I approached, I allowed him to read in my face that something was wrong. He began to twist his new ring as I spoke. What I described was the very last thing he expected. Tears poured down his cheeks. We were alone then, but I knew not for long. I found a quiet and empty room nearby where we just sat together, neither one saying much for a while.

Then he began to ask more about Down's syndrome babies. He wanted to know what they looked like, so I described their physical characteristics. To his question about how it happens I explained that it is a genetic, chromosomal problem. Then came the ultimate, shattering news.

"You mean retarded?" he asked. "Mentally retarded? Oh, Doc, oh no. Oh, God, no!..

There was a pause, a very long pause. Then he said, "What you are telling me is he'll never go to college. Is that what you're saying, Doctor?"

Bill and Melinda were never able to accept or cope with their exceptional child. People tried to help them, but the grief, the dashing of expectations, was just too great. Their "imperfect" baby (imperfect only by human standards) died a few weeks later.

I saw Melinda in the office at her six-weeks checkup. She never vented her feelings except to say that "he is far better off in heaven than down here."

Only one thing healed their wounds — the delivery fifteen months later of a beautiful, blond baby. And when he delivered, the nurses were able to say, "Oh, he's just perfect!" I predicted to myself then that one day this second child would probably look just like Dad and wear a college graduation ring, just like Dad.

When their Down's baby died, most said it was a blessing. But I have often wondered what effect that "imperfect" child would have had on their lives and their marriage had he lived. Would he have caused them to seek after God for help? Would their marriage have been stronger as they worked together to raise the child? If so, the tragedy would really have been a blessing. Unfortunately, we will never know. Today Melinda and Bill are divorced and their second child, the "perfect" one, is just another victim of joint custody.

You see, this couple could not cope, for they could not understand. They did not have the ability to see the spiritual meaning in all that happened. They didn't even know that God always takes care of His children and everything brought into our lives is for our good.

Kathy Swanson delivered her baby at 4 A.M. It was a rather routine labor and delivery, but the baby demonstrated some mongoloid features at birth. The diagnosis was not clear-cut, however, the baby boy cried and had good tone and color. Suspicion is not enough. Therefore, no mention was made regarding the possibility of Down's syndrome.

Confirmation would have to come from the pediatricians. Kathy herself did not notice any of the unusual features when the nurse brought the baby to her all neatly wrapped in warm blankets. Kathy's husband, Steve, was also unaware as he peered through the nursery window twenty minutes later.

At 8:30 the same morning, the pediatrician reviewed Kathy's chart in the hallway before entering her room. He did not look forward to the task that lay ahead. In her prenatal record he noticed her husband's occupation listed as a seminary student. He interpreted that to mean the couple was "religious." He would keep that in mind.

Physicians are not immune to ineptness, as his opening sentence would prove. In the practice of medicine, explaining unpleasant findings accurately and gently is an art. Some doctors are less artistic than others.

After introducing himself to Kathy (Steve was then at home sleeping after being up all night), the pediatrician sat down next to the bed. "Mrs. Swanson, I'm afraid God has played a trick on you," he said.

(Now, I can't for the life of me understand why he said that, but he did. It probably was an attempt to acknowledge the Swansons' religious background, but it was hopelessly inappropriate. God uses every situation, however, every sentence for a reason. This was no exception.

Many months later Kathy recounted to me the entirety of that conversation. She told me it was the opening remark that helped her accept what came next. As a Christian, she knew God never plays tricks or makes mistakes. It was the blatant inaccuracy of the doctor's statement that gave her the confidence she could handle whatever bad news the doctor would bring.)

The young physician continued, "I'm sorry, I did not mean it quite that way. I meant only to say that there is a problem with your baby. We believe he is a Down's syndrome child. In the past it has been called mongolism. Are you at all familiar with the term?"

Kathy nodded.

"Of course, we will be doing some chromosome studies to verify it, but I believe there is no question about the diagnosis at this point. I want to explain the situation to you and answer any questions you may have. The nurse said your husband is at home now, but I'll be happy to go over it again with him later today. I know how difficult all this must be for you."

Kathy remained composed as she listened, although tears kept filling and refilling her eyes. The pediatrician carefully and thoroughly explained how there is a wide range of physical and mental capabilities with these children. Only in time would they know at what level their son would be able to function. He encouraged Kathy to raise the baby in their home and outlined the various assisting services that would be available to her.

After the doctor left, Kathy called Steve. He arrived almost immediately. They clutched each other as she related all the doctor had said.

Steve and Kathy hurt. They hurt bad. But their faith remained strong. Steve said, "Honey, remember in the labor room last night, we dedicated our child to God. We said if it were a son we would name him David. I know He has given him to us for a special reason, and we must praise Him for it." And they did.

Steve next called his parents to tell them their new grandchild had been born with Down's syndrome. Then he broke down and cried.

Kathy and Steve later told me that one of the greatest comforts they received during those difficult days was the support of Christian friends who rallied around them, loved them, helped them and prayed for them.

That support started immediately in the hospital. The Lord gave Kathy two Christian nurses who were able to meet both her spiritual and her physical needs. "Bear one another's burdens, and thus fulfill the law of Christ" (Galatians 6:2).

Neither Kathy nor Steve ever asked the question, "Why me?" They knew God's goodness, His love and His sovereignty. They praised Him for placing David in their home, where he could be assured of receiving maximum love.

Quickly God allowed this faithful couple to see how He would use them to help others. Like a ripple effect, the birth of David was to touch other members of His family.

Steve was an adult Sunday school teacher at the time. Four of the couples in his class were expecting babies. Within weeks of David's birth, one of them also had a Down's syndrome baby.

Another Christian friend of the Swansons was at her own baby shower when she heard about Kathy's delivery. As she and her husband drove home that night, they discussed together what their reaction would be if it happened to them. Even before they arrived home, her labor began. Six hours later she also delivered a Down's syndrome baby.

Both these couples admit it was the unyielding strength they saw in Kathy and Steve Swanson that played a major role in their own ability to cope.

Coincidence? No, not coincidence. In just a matter of weeks, God ministered to many of His children using a unique child named David.

And what about that boy today? Well, he's six at the time of this writing and has two sisters and one brother. What do they say about David? "Oh, we love David. He's fun. And he's always happy."

Two couples, Melinda and Bill, Kathy and Steve, shared common "tragedies." The first couple asked, "Why us?" Living only with human standards and worldly hope, they had no resources upon which to call. The only solution to their misfortune was a replacement.

The second couple did not need to ask, "Why us?" They knew there was a reason. They did not have to accept the calamity with simple resignation because "it was God's will." It was much deeper and more practical than that. They survived because they believed the scriptural promise of Romans 8:28. God's written Word gave them spiritual insight to look beyond the immediate situation. They knew their David had been given to them for a definite reason. And that reason was *for their ultimate good.*

Suffering and Crisis — God's Tools

People without Christ who live in accordance with man's wisdom alone do well as long as things go smoothly. But when personal tragedy strikes, they often fall apart. Some even react with bitterness and resentment. God gets the blame ironically, the same God in whom there had been no prior interest.

God does not cause suffering, but He does allow it, and we saw earlier how crisis is one way God brings people to Himself. Why does God permit these things to happen to His children, to Christians? There are at least four reasons.

One reason for our suffering is to equip us to comfort others during their times of trouble. We share best what we have personally experienced. It is a tough way to prepare for a lesson, but it is the best teaching we'll ever do.

Kathy and Steve traveled down a terrifying road, but it gave them the credentials to speak authoritatively on the subject. Since David's birth, that couple — the entire family — has had a personal ministry to so many others who have also been called to parent a Down's child. Every one of us knows the reassuring feeling that comes from just talking to someone who has gone through and survived the same ordeal we are facing.

A second reason for tribulation in a believer's life is to promote our Christian growth. Problems are one of the best ways to stimulate individual maturity. Parenthood is a good example of this principle. If parents were to give their children everything they desired and shield them from any personal trials, they would surely become spoiled, ungrateful brats. God does not want this to happen to His children.

When our spiritual growth gets bogged down (often when we begin placing too much emphasis on material things), God will send us a hardship "reminder" designed to get our eyes back on Him and off the comforts of this world. We may call it unfair, but He calls it chastening. "Those whom the Lord loves He disciplines" (Hebrews 12:6).

A third reason for our suffering is to teach us how to be patient and calm in times of crisis. God does not want His children to crumble under pressure. He wants us "hanging in there," enduring, as the Bible calls it, both for our own good and for our example to others.

The presence of the Holy Spirit in us is the power that makes this kind of response possible. "Consider it all joy, my brethren, when you encounter various trials, knowing that the testing of your faith produces endurance" (James 1:2-3).

And, of course, suffering is part of our lives for contrast —to heighten our appreciation for things to come. It pleases me that God, the Great Obstetrician, has selected labor and delivery to illustrate this important spiritual concept. As Jesus' time on earth was nearing an end, He gathered His disciples together to explain His imminent death. Our Lord used the analogy of childbirth:

> The world will greatly rejoice over what is going to happen to me, and you will weep. But your weeping shall suddenly be turned to wonderful joy [when you see me again]. It will be the same joy as that of a woman in labor when her child is born —her anguish gives place to rapturous joy and the pain is forgotten (John 16:20–21, TLB).

In order to savor fully the infinite peace that awaits us in heaven, we must first taste the bitterness of affliction here on earth. "God has reserved for his children the priceless gift of eternal life. . . . There is wonderful joy ahead, even though the going is rough for a while down here" (1 Peter 1:4,6, TLB).

Trials, tribulation, suffering —they are never easy, never pleasant. We all want to avoid them. But once we understand why, once we are able to see clearly their purpose and benefit, it is a lot easier to get through them.

This kind of insight can come only from God. It is given to us only after we experience new birth. It is a *very special prize.*

ten

More Prizes

Perhaps the most satisfying prize of spiritual birth is a clean conscience. Driving to New Mexico on a family ski trip, I noticed the speedometer occasionally creeping above the posted fifty-five speed limit. During those times of excess, I had to spend most of my time peering into the rearview mirror, scanning for state police cars.

What a perfect illustration of the need for a clean conscience, I thought to myself. When we live according to God's rules, within His "speed limits," we can devote more time to real living and less time to worrying about getting caught. It conserves energy, if nothing else. One who is obedient to the Lord need not waste time looking in the rear-view mirror.

A married friend of mine best illustrates the satisfying peace of a clean conscience. Two years ago he nearly ruined his life. It all started when he began to travel with the wrong crowd. Every working day ended with "the boys" at a nearby restaurant bar.

Before long, time with the boys merged (as it so often does) into time with "the girls." His marriage began to crumble as he went from one affair to another. Life became one complicated coverup after another, sneaking around, lying, and, of course, always having to remember what he said. Even time at home was a constant vigil to conceal from his wife unexpected telephone calls from his girl-friends.

Through a series of his own preparatory events, a trip to God's delivery room and a loving and forgiving Christian wife and daughter, he came to his senses just in time.

Now clearly the spiritual leader of his own home, he is growing and maturing in the Lord by leaps and bounds. One thing I notice is the faithful way he gives God credit for restoring his life. Describing the luxury of a clean conscience, he jests, "Now when I'm at home, I can actually let my wife answer the telephone!"

Another priceless benefit of new birth is companionship, a special kind of relationship that sees Jesus Christ becoming our best friend. It is an intimate friendship with one who knows everything about us, yet accepts and loves us just the way we are.

Our new companion is dependable. He never

lets us down. He is always available so we can talk to Him whenever we wish. He has even promised never to leave us or forsake us (Hebrews 13:5).

Together this friend and I can do anything. He enables me to cope with frustration, even to love when loving seems unreasonable. He makes it possible to survive a week that sees a bank account overdrawn, the car breaking down, the IRS announcing an audit, the house getting burglarized, and a rebelling child testing the limits. Nothing is too great for Him. He comforts me, encourages me, counsels and guides me. That is some kind of friend.

A third exciting prize of rebirth is the accessibility of Scripture. "Thy Word is a lamp to my feet, and a light to my path" (Psalm 119:105). The door to this treasure house is flung wide open by the Holy Spirit the instant we receive Christ. He is the essential enzyme, the catalyst, converting God's written Word into a handbook for day-to-day living.

Looking back, one of the things I appreciate most is the impact Jesus Christ has had in our home. That could have happened only by my becoming aware of my correct role as spiritual leader of the family.

As mentioned earlier, the Bible was my counselor in this area. It outlined clearly the proper relationship I was to have with my wife. I am to:

love her. . . . . Ephesians 5:25-33
live with her for life . . . . . Matthew 19:3-9

be faithful to her . . . .   Malachi 2:14-15
be satisfied with her . . . . .   Proverbs 5:18-19
instruct her . . . .   1 Corinthians 14:34-35
honor her . . . .   1 Peter 3:7
confer with her . . . .   Genesis 31:4-16
provide for her . . . .   1 Timothy 5:8

Moreover, the Bible listed my responsibilities to my children. I am not to provoke them (Ephesians 6:4), but rather to:

love them . . . .   Genesis 37:4
instruct them . . . .   Proverbs 1:8
guide and warn them . . . .   1 Thessalonians 2:11
train them . . . .   Hosea 11:3
rebuke them . . . .   Genesis 34:30
restrain them . . . .   1 Samuel 3:13
punish them . . . .   Deuteronomy 21:18-21
discipline them . . . .   Hebrews 12:7
nourish them . . . .   Isaiah 1:2
supply their needs . . . . . .   Matthew 7:8-11

(These references come from the "Biblical Cyclopedic Index" in the *Open Bible*, Nashville: Thomas Nelson.)

The Bible is also our faithful friend during difficult times, and even in times of tragedy, as it was for one of my patients Viola, a young, Christian mother, faced a severe test. Her twin boys were the delight of her life. I was there when she delivered them, and they were gorgeous. The praises Viola gave the Lord in the delivery room were heartfelt and profuse; it is one birth I shall never forget.

When the twins were just months old, she took them with her one day to one of the nearby shopping malls. While there, one of the twins slipped and fell, hitting his head. It was a freak accident, but the cerebral injury was critical. For over a week, the toddler lay unconcious in intensive care.

When the baby died, the young mother was grief stricken. Later in my office she told me about those difficult times. "It was the longest eight days of my life. I prayed and prayed for God to let Jason live, but He didn't. One of my friends gave me a passage in the Bible that really helped, 2 Samuel, the twelfth chapter. It is the story of King David and what he went through when his young son died, and his reaction. It was just what I needed.

"You know, Dr. Wells, if I didn't have God, if I didn't have Jesus, if I didn't have the Bible, I never would have made it."

Eternal Life

There are many other rich delivery room prizes, but the greatest of all has to be life after death — with God forever! Our physical birthday usually grants only eighty years or so of living. But our spiritual birthday guarantees an eternity. I guess that best explains why this obstetrician is more concerned about spiritual birth than physical birth.

Heaven is the greatest trophy of all. How often I have wished the Bible described it in greater detail. However, Scripture does tell us all we need to know—and heaven is one fantastic place to live. It is where we finally witness first-hand the fullness of God's glory. What an experience that will be!

Since none of us has seen heaven and returned to give an eyewitness account, some find it difficult to get excited about it. One patient with terminal cancer had only a few weeks to live. One day when I was on my rounds, she told me about a conversation she had experienced with her roommate. It seems the roommate had told her just how it was possible to go to heaven by believing in Jesus.

"Heaven is not what concerns me, Dr. Wells," the woman said. Battling for her life, she was pale and emaciated. "I'm scared. I need help *right now*. I want to get well *now*. I want God to cure the cancer. I don't even want to think about going to heaven. I want to think about earth."

Her response was quite natural. It is true that going to heaven requires we first taste death (unless the Lord comes first). And death does hold an aura of fear. Little wonder that "right now" is so important to us.

But "now" can never be fulfilling until we are right with God. There can be no personal peace here on earth until we have total assurance about our destination after we die. "Right now" takes care of itself only after the issue of "then" is settled.

Don't Put It Off

A clean conscience, partnership with Jesus Christ, the wisdom of Scripture and eternal life: these prizes belong to those who seek and find a personal relationship with Jesus Christ.

Only God can inject meaning into life. Only He can rekindle a marriage growing cold. Only the Savior can give peace and happiness in exchange for misery and frustration. Only Jesus offers this new life.

But it must begin with new birth. Don't put it off. Go now to *His* hospital, to *His* obstetrical suite, and be born again. Receive new birth; receive new life.